Praise for *Two Faces* ~~of the Moon~~

"What the noisy and perilous world needs now is Carolyn McGrath's fervent paean to solitude. In *Two Faces of the Moon*, our companions are not only the author in her beloved wilderness, but the ghosts of the remarkable women who nurtured and protected it. Their stories, along with McGrath's moving personal journey, give this memoir its distinct power and relevance."
—Christopher Castellani, author of *Leading Men*.

"Carolyn McGrath tells an unusual but compelling story of her life as the owner of a small island in a Canadian lake where one summer, helped by her surroundings of outstanding natural beauty, she looked at her complex relationship with her family and worked out who she was; and where now, the great spoiling tide of the 21st century is fast approaching. Her memoir is a beautifully-written, passionate and lyrical testament to the worth of the natural world which is everywhere so threatened."
—Michael McCarthy, author of
The Moth Snowstorm – Nature and Joy

"*Two Faces of the Moon* is at once an intensely personal memoir and a resonant meditation on the complex relationships between children and parents, the role of humans in nature, and the precious pleasures of solitude. Throughout, Carolyn McGrath writes with a deep and loving sense of place that leaves one wishing for their own island refuge in the wilderness."
—Andrea L. Smalley, author of *Wild By*
Nature: North American Animals Confront
Colonization and *The Market in Birds: Commercial*
Hunting, Conservation, and the Origins of Wildlife
Consumerism.

"Virginia Woolf said every woman needs a room of her own to write. For Carolyn McGrath, the room is an island of her own on a lake in Canada where she spends summers with two dogs in close company with the local wildlife. In this moving and beautifully written book, she comes to terms with her feelings for her mother, dying in a nursing home nearby, and for her long-deceased father, who had entered this wilderness with a gun. She also describes the lives of her lifelong neighbors, descended from 19th century pioneers who forged a living in the backwoods surrounding the lake. In an Afterword, she recounts the inevitable and threatening changes coming to this once remote and isolated Eden."

—E. A. M. Jakab, author of *Louis Pasteur: Hunting Killer Germs,* and *The Halloween Party*

"This absorbing book is a work of art, exploring natural beauty, solitude, and the mysteries of parental influence. I enjoyed it immensely."

—Adele Glimm, author of *Rachel Carson: Protecting our Earth* and *Gene Hunter: The Story of Neuropsychologist Nancy Wexler.*

"Beautifully remembered story of life at the author's beloved island cottage. Of special interest to Bobs Lake residents, local history fans and anyone who cares deeply about the natural world."

—Peri McQuay, author of *Singing Meadow: The Adventure of Creating a Country Home* and *A Wing in the Door: Life with a Red-Tailed Hawk.*

TWO FACES
OF THE
MOON

A SMALL ISLAND MEMOIR

CAROLYN MCGRATH

Brandylane
Publishers, Inc.
Publishing books since 1985

ISBN: 978-1-958754-33-7
Library of Congress Control Number: 2022924091

Designed by Sami Langston
Project managed by Grace Albritton

Printed in the United States of America

Published by
Brandylane Publishers, Inc.
5 S. 1st Street
Richmond, Virginia 23219

Brandylane
Publishers, Inc.
Publishing books since 1985

brandylanepublishers.com

For Daughters and their Mothers everywhere.

He wanted an island all of his own: not necessarily to be alone on it, but to make it a world of his own. An island, if it is big enough, is no better than a continent. It has to be really quite small before it feels like an island; and this story will show how tiny it has to be before you can presume to fill it with your own personality.

—D. H. Lawrence, *The Man Who Loved Islands*

Preface

Age makes us all wanderers in time, searchers of the thickets of our pasts where things occurred that seemed to have little or no significance at the time but now, we suspect, had everything to do with defining us. We dig in the rich loam of memories that come to us as images and stories. A memoir must have truth in it, but when things deemed important have to be made to fit together somehow in order to become a narrative, it may end up feeling like fiction, as though the writer is creating a character, someone she can manipulate and ultimately judge and embrace—or disassociate from. What we write should make sense, but life doesn't always make sense. We strive for a conclusion when we haven't come to a conclusion yet. Writing any book can be like walking a very big dog on a leash. You own her, but she controls you and determines where you go.

I've chosen to write about a place that has become, over the years, the psychic landscape for one of my personas. The place is an island, all my own and very small, but the thing about islands is that they don't limit you to their parameters. From this island of mine I can look out across vast distances of water and sky and other lives, and fall down the rabbit hole of time looking for me. The persona travelling with two dogs along the path in this book comes to a humbling discovery.

This book has been a very big dog.

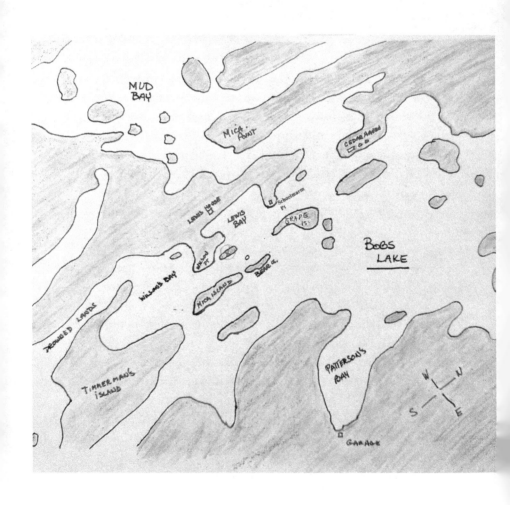

Introduction

What an entry I made. Someone cut my mother open, and I was lifted into the world unsullied by the normal push and pull. Pink Perfect, all nine pounds and thirteen ounces of me. My parents called me "Pinky" for years. I had no rivals. During my mother's first attempt two years before, they'd let her labor until she nearly died, then took out a poor broken baby boy who died the following day. She was told never to have another, but she faced the risk to have me.

My mother was thirty-six and my father forty-seven when I arrived. He'd already had a daughter in a different marriage twenty years earlier. My mother clearly thought only a boy would do for my dad this time, but somehow, he managed to rally enthusiasm for another little girl child. She wrote to her brother at the time:

When they told me I had a girl, I was so disappointed I nearly cried. Then I thought, What a silly thing to do if she is as nice a baby as they say. And when they showed her to me, I fell for her flat! She is such a fat pretty thing. I was afraid of how Phil would feel, but when he came to see me in the evening, his face and eyes were beaming, and I knew he felt as I did.

I'm hard pressed to say whether, as fathers go, mine was good or not. I can say that mine went a long way in forming me as a person. I had my dad for only seventeen years. He was a chiropractor and his office was in our house, our living room his waiting room, so he was always there monitoring my life. I was often told that I was like him. Such was the strength of my attraction to this idea that I felt unfairly dismayed sometimes when I could not deny certain traits I owed to my mother. The question is why I would want to be like a troubled man, an alcoholic, a heavy smoker, a war veteran whose great talent for cussing often caused my mother to cover my ears. A father who clearly wished he'd had a son instead.

One who taught me to box and shoot a gun. After his death, my young mind cleansed him of faults, and he became someone I was determined to be proud of.

Memoirs often evoke tragedy, abuse, the ever-challenging truth of human existence, the "miracle of miracles" the author represents in having overcome her lousy childhood. Frank McCourt, in beginning his memoir, *Angela's Ashes*, wrote, "It was, of course, a miserable childhood: the happy childhood is hardly worth your while."

Writing about an alcoholic parent usually documents cruelty, shame, and neglect. If you wonder how Frank McCourt and his brothers could weep with love for a father who could tell his boys he loved them while he left them to starve, drinking every penny that ever came their way and disappearing so that he would not have to face their misery, I'll tell you that while I can't compete with the McCourts for a miserable Irish childhood, I understand that love. I was ashamed when my mother had to go out to Ray's Bar and bring my dad home, but both she and I loved him. Somehow, he had the kind of real estate of the soul that gives a person ballast, something to which another person can anchor a strong attachment, but his temper, or frequent loss of it, caused me to expect great roller coaster rides in life, and it took me years after his death to coast out flat.

My most indelible memories of him are from time spent on our small island in Canada, where I can walk in his footprints all these years later. He left it to me, and it became a shrine to his memory, where I've been dancing with his ghost every summer of my adult life, much to the chagrin of my husband.

As a writer, I've found my dad's essence difficult to capture. I'm reminded of my maternal grandmother's observation: "Men are like fleas. Just when you think you have your thumb on them, they're gone." It wasn't until the year 2001, the year when my poor, ninety-six-year-old mother was dying, that I began to unravel the puzzle of my relationship with my parents. By then I was learning that strong people can have great weaknesses, and that people perceived to be weak can have hidden powers of strength and endurance.

Summer 2001

1

My husband has told me that people think I'm "strange." No other wife of our acquaintance turns her back upon a beautiful suburban home with a swimming pool, leaving friends, colleagues—and husband!—to spend her summers in the backwoods alone. It's five in the morning in early June when I leave our house on Long Island with my black lab, Blue, and drive five hundred miles north to Bobs Lake, in Ontario.

Blue has known for days that we were headed for Canada, reading all the signs of my coming departure. The first thing she does when we arrive at the garage on the lake is to wade directly into the water up to her shoulders, drink deeply, swim out and back, then shake water all over me, roll on the bank with her legs in the air, and disappear into the woods, to return only when called. Meanwhile I slide my work boat into the water—the same boat that, many years ago, capsized in this very bay with four people and a dog in it. The dog died.

That was then. This old boat and I understand each other now. I lift the 10 hp motor out of the car and onto its transom and load my gear. When I'm ready to leave, I call Blue, designating her place in the boat. As usual she doesn't like it, trampling bags and boxes and shifting her weight from side to side.

Bobs Lake is a dammed lake, a major reservoir for the complex water system that feeds the historic Rideau Canal, a UNESCO World Heritage site run by National Parks Canada. Because this is flooded, hilly country, there are many islands and bays within bays, giving the lake much more shoreline than if you drew a smooth circle around nine thousand acres of water; namely, two hundred kilometers of shoreline for a lake only sixteen kilometers in length. The shores lining the lake are a mix of conifer and deciduous trees, dark green, broken here and there by brilliant white slashes of paper birch. We motor out of the bay into the main channel and a mild chop, Blue standing high on a duffel bag as though piloting us, the wind lifting her ears straight out to the side, flapping like wings.

Through a pass, we enter a narrower channel where the Lewis farm can be seen on a hill above their bay. The mainland forms arms around the water as though to gather the riches of the lake in toward them. There is no road access to the farm, which is itself almost entirely surrounded by water. My island lies off the southern arm.

The thrill I feel on seeing the small island, of knowing I've made the journey and will once again inhabit the old log cabin, has never lost its power. The place has its history. In the 1920s a man named Wilson from Hamilton, Ontario, was looking for land in the wilderness and bought the southern peninsula arm from the Lewises. According to Hugh Lewis, eighteen men came by boat or barge to build a lodge and outbuildings, including a boathouse over the water with servants' quarters above it.

In 1926, on the half-acre island off their shore, the Wilsons built the log cabin as a playhouse retreat for their daughter, Marian. The walls and overhead beams of the cabin's main room are twenty-foot virgin-forest white cedar logs of uniform width, impossible to find now.

Wilson's wealth was dazzling to the few people living here on the lake in those days. According to Hugh Lewis, whom they'd hired as overseer, the family was chauffeured in Pierce-Arrow town cars and limousines. There was rumored to be gold on the door handles of the house at Hamilton. He said that they vacationed in Bermuda in the winter, and opened the lodge here on Bobs Lake in May, where they would stay off and on during the summer. Wilson installed his own Delco system for electricity, and it was said that people came from miles around to see the lights. There was indoor plumbing in the lodge, another oddity here in the backwoods, where pipes could freeze before the woodstove was restoked on winter mornings. The Wilsons brought two Chinese cooks, some maids, and a man to stay year-around on the lake to tend the foxes they kept for hunting. Maids would carry meals from the lodge across a footbridge to Marian and her friends on the island.

With the stock market crash of 1929, the Wilsons lost their wealth. Not long afterward, all the buildings on the mainland were destroyed in a fire. After Wilson died, Hugh Lewis bought back the peninsula from the widow for a cow pasture, as well as the Wilsons' garage on the eastern shore of the lake where I park my car. Marian's playhouse on the island was spared from the fire, and in 1937 my dad bought island and cabin for $400.

The cabin faces east, in front of it a floating dock chained to the island. In the high water of spring, wind has driven one corner of it up onto the rocky shore. Blue is out before we're secured, unsure which direction to head in first, making fast starts, then changing her mind, nose to the ground.

When I've tied up, I lever the corner of the dock off the rocks with an iron bar, then span the breach with the long plank catwalk leaning against the cabin. In the breeze, the grasses along the bank bend in waves, as though a hand were passing over them. With the bags of groceries out of the sun on the large screened porch, I unlock the cabin's wide front door and step into the cedary smell of the main room. I'm home.

Once I have the power switched on, refrigerator plugged in, shutters open, gear moved in, and my bed made up, I take a broom to the outhouse, a short walk up a path to the north. The island is too small for the extensive septic system required for indoor plumbing. Anyway, I love the fact that this old outhouse draws me out to see and hear things happening on the lake and island that I might otherwise miss. It's not called the "call of nature" for nothing.

After sweeping out the webs, spiders running for cover, I sit on the wooden seat, door open but screened from view by a wooden lattice. On the wall in a frame is a cartoon that my dad drew, brown and faded now. In it, a voluptuous woman in a red dress is draped on a log on shore while her husband, in waders, fishes in a stream. She calls to him: *"Darling, would I be more fascinating if I ate worms?"*

Back inside the cabin, Blue stares at me until I rummage through packed boxes to find some dog food. I can't keep going without food either, so I open a can and heat soup on the old four-burner kerosene stove, tilting one of the chimneys to light the wick. No gourmet food here while I'm alone. I revert to the simple menus of my youth.

Before dark, I leave Blue in the cabin and motor over to the Lewis farm to draw some drinking water from their well and pick up Ring, their border collie. Ring is named for the ring of long pure-white hair, like an Elizabethan ruff, around the neck of his otherwise black-haired body. From his chain-dragged circle of dirt at the top of the steep, grassy hill, he locks his eyes to mine as I climb up to the house. "Yes," I tell him, but first I go to the house.

I've known the Lewis family all my life. Each May and October my dad brought other men to the lake for ten days of hunting and fishing. On the first of these trips, he saw Hugh Lewis rowing past the dock in a flat-bottomed boat. Everyone called him Hughie, a lean man, skin tanned to leather, eyes the color of the sky. My dad waved him in.

Hughie had no motor in those days and rowed everywhere. He'd broken a leg on the ice during the previous winter and it wasn't mending. My dad, a chiropractor, put his hands on it to feel the break and found that it needed to be reset. Hughie had it done and the leg was fine. From then on, my dad became known on the lake as "Doc."

That began one of those strong male friendships that strike sparks. He and Hughie were together every day while my dad was at the lake. Almost everything they said made them laugh.

In the summers, while I was growing up, we'd hear the splash of nets at dawn in Lewis Bay as Hughie seined for the minnows he'd sell to fishermen from his dock. When he had his catch, he'd row to the island for breakfast, bringing cream and butter from the farm. My mother would serve up pancakes or bacon and eggs. Sometimes Hughie would join us for supper as well, and then he'd take us fishing. Fish were very plentiful in the lake in those days, and the next night we'd eat a "mess" of what they called "pan fish": smallmouth bass, rock bass, perch, or bluegills. If they didn't stop fishing when the sun set, the bullheads would begin to bite, and we would sometimes eat their softer, red flesh.

While Hughie could neither read nor write, he used language fluidly, creatively, telling stories that grew with each telling, pausing in the places that deserved appreciation for the humor, laughing with a hand to his mouth to hide missing teeth. During his all-male expeditions, my dad relied on Hughie to join in, guide them on the lake, and enhance their experience with his character. Eat and drink and cuss and fish and kill, tell stories and laugh; they did it all with gusto. And sometimes another local man named Joe Green would join them, and they'd laugh because if Joe went home drunk, his wife would make him sleep in the pig pen. Of course, she was crazy . . . she'd sweep their island with a broom. Hilarious.

Over the years, other summer people on the lake probably thought my dad had *gone native*. He had, preferring while here to seek the locals' charm and knowledge of the lake. At our home in Ohio, I never heard him laugh the way he did on Bobs Lake, where the deep sound of it warmed me.

When I was very young, while Hughie guided them fishing in the evenings, my parents would leave me on the farm with his wife, Lizzie. She tells me that I was a baby sleeping on her bed when she went into labor with her daughter, Joan, who became my lifelong friend. Hughie died years ago, and Lizzie has moved into town to be near Joan. Their son, Ervin, now owns the farm.

Tonight, the Lewises are watching television and don't hear me coming until I knock on the kitchen door. Ervin's wife, June, greets me with a smile, urging me to come in. She and Ervin have worked for years at Nordlaw Lodge at the north end of the lake. June is the pastry chef, and Ervin is their fishing guide and handyman. I don't want to interrupt their program, so I stay just a moment, but Ervin comes outside to help me fill my five-gallon container at the spigot. He asks about my mother. I ask about his.

I'm here for a long stay this year because west of here, beyond Crow Lake and along the shores of Sharbot Lake, my ninety-six-year-old mother, Dorothea, is sitting in the parlor of a seniors' home, her old head nodding with confused imaginings. I make monthly drives all year long from New York to Sharbot Lake to spend weekends with her. Because I'm a teacher with summers free, now that I'm here I'll make the hour's drive to see her every third day, weather permitting.

I decline Ervin's offer to carry my water container down the hill and ask if I can take Ring. As always, he says "Sure, it will be good for him," and finds a leash I'll never use. Ervin has explained that he can't let Ring run free. Border collies insist on working. They're bred for sheep, but Ervin raises cattle. Ring is too good a herder for cows. He herds them into a tight bunch until they look like a wagon train drawn into a circle, horns out and rear quarters backed in for protection against his nips. These cows don't need such supervision.

Unchained, Ring is down the steep hill and into my boat before I can take two steps with my heavy load. The first time I brought him to the island, he tucked himself under my arm as we rode and pressed himself against me, trembling with excitement. Nowadays he rides the bow, his feet on the gunwale, one side, then the other, as though to urge our craft through the waves. The sun is falling behind the hill. East above the islands the clouds take on a rosy hue, and, overhead, birds fly from the lake toward the west in pairs. The moon is up, stretching her arms, surveying the lake and turning up her wattage with the promise of darkness.

Ring does a good job of marking the island as I tie up, then waits by the door for me to release Blue. Even though Blue was spayed early in life, Ring is always ready to practice his skill at seduction. He kisses her and nips her ears, while she feints and rolls, loving the attention. They couldn't be more different. Blue is big, like her black Lab father, and her fur is short and glossy, with a mane of thick spiky hairs around her shoulders that stands up to make her appear larger and fierce when she's afraid. Ring, with his long fine hair, looks bigger than he is, his lean, hard body smaller underneath. As Ervin puts it, "He's all hair and bones." Ring is never afraid.

The Author with Ring and Blue.

2

It's dark when a concert of loon voices begins—high maniacal laughter and some insistent yodels. I dress for bed and sit in the living room at the round red and black table. The wood floors of the cabin have always been painted yellow, a popular floor color for dark Ontario kitchens in the old days.

A stranger would be hard pressed to understand the cabin's décor. Marian Wilson's gaily painted "playhouse" furniture from the 1920s, including a hutch with colorful teacups, contrasts with my dad's hunting lodge paraphernalia: dusty old posters of hunting parties on the walls and shutters, framed pictures of wildlife and hunting dogs, big snapping turtle shells on the hearth, and a whole corner devoted to fishing rods and tackle boxes. Nailed up on either side of the chimney are a pair of Hugh Lewis's old mended snowshoes. "The Angler's Prayer," tacked on a bedroom door, reads:

Lord give me grace to catch a fish
So big that even I
When talking of it afterwards
May never need to lie.

What a mishmash. Yet the primary colors somehow connect the precious and the primal. Marian's blood-red paint goes together with guns and dead animals, after all. The bright colors of her curtains, rugs, and flags pull together the reds and darker colors in the room and the yellow of the floor, forming a bright mosaic. It's vibrant and fun-loving and savage. For years I've kept everything just as it was during my childhood, choosing to preserve it as it was left to me.

My mother used to sit at the table in the midst of it all and play solitaire. Her cards are old and gummy, but I deal a hand and surprise myself by winning the first time. I'm observed in this victory on three sides by moth-eaten deer heads mounted on the log walls.

***

It's hard to escape the saying "You can never go home again." Thomas Wolfe made it the title of a novel, and in *A Death in the Family*, the author James Agee wrote: "How far we all come away from ourselves. So far, so much between, you can never go home again." Then there's Maya Angelou's response: "You can never go home again, but the truth is you can never leave home, so it's all right." The trick is to have two homes and never really leave either. I leave home to come home every summer and find it just the same.

When my parents first traveled here, they'd been married only three years. A policeman in our hometown of Kent, Ohio, had been fishing on this lake and told my dad about an island for sale. It was during the Great Depression, and the cop couldn't afford to buy it. My dad bought it sight unseen, and he and my mother set off for Ontario one evening and drove all night to see their new purchase. Because my dad was a terrible driver, she drove most of the time. The next morning, they crossed the St. Lawrence River by ferry at the Thousand Islands, where there was not yet a bridge. My mother wrote to her brother that the roads near Bobs Lake were "winding, rutted and ungraded dirt. It took more than an hour to go fifteen miles." At the lake they rented a boat at a fishing camp and followed directions to the island they'd just bought. They found the cabin derelict. The porch screens were torn, so they measured the windows and drove over the fifteen miles of washboard road to the town of Westport, where they could buy new screen and order a mattress to be delivered. They spent that night at the fishing camp, and the next day, with the help of the man named Joe Green, they replaced the screens.

In that letter she wrote that the screens were replaced "so we wouldn't be eaten by mosquitoes that night. However, we were, for the mosquitoes were already in!" She also wrote that Joe Green was half "Indian," part of the romance of this adventure for her.

They put their new mattress on the floor. Then it began to rain.

...and the longer it rained the harder it seemed to come down and pretty soon the roof leaked everywhere it could think of. We rolled up the mattress and put it in the front room, for the bedroom was raining in like a sieve. We kept mopping up water there and still it was about an inch high at the door sill.

But the roof leaked into the front room as well, and the next day it continued to rain. "It would stop for a while and then pour like blazes!" So, they made another bumpy thirty-mile round trip to Westport to order roofing paper delivered. Once again they hired Joe Green, and he and his son Clint helped my dad put the roof on the cabin. My mother had to drive to Westport yet again, this time taking a suffering Clint to have a tooth pulled.

When I was young, it seemed to me that my mother shared my father's enthusiasm for all this, that the anticipation and excitement about our summer trips to the island were generated by the two of them, but I wonder now if she wished not to return after that first visit. In her letter she wrote that when my dad heard frogs at the garage landing:

"Phil got a club and tried to club a few so we might try frog legs for a treat but they were quicker than he and someday we shall go over there with a line *and a bit of red flannel and just see if we don't have frog legs. Phil will have to clean them, tho, I'm thinking!"*

I'm sure that she had never imagined eating frogs, but it wasn't long before my father developed his strategy of shooting them with his .22 rifle and she learned to clean and cook them. The tongue-in-cheek tone of her letter to her brother suggests that she was merely tolerant of my dad's whims, hiding it well, being a good sport. Phil sank into it head over heels, and that meant that she, so in love with Phil, had to as well.

* * *

Ring accompanies me on the short walk up the path north to the outhouse. The moon has travelled west and blinks her hand-me-down light through the trees as I walk. Returning, I pause at the dock to see the heavens at night without the smog and light pollution of the metropolitan area of New York. Here the sky is full of bright stars. A brilliant Milky Way sweeps overhead, barely missing Cygnus, the swan. In my younger days I was uneasy about being here on the island alone at night. I gave my dad's rifle to Ervin long ago, but I'd sometimes take a kitchen knife into the bedroom at night and keep it within reach, especially when fishermen just off shore made occasional splashes or bumps in the dark.

As I grew older, I lost that fear, influenced by Simone de Beauvoir, who, in her memoirs, points out that if a woman is afraid to be alone, that fear will curtail her privacy, her ability to explore the world for herself, and her time for the kind of meditative thinking that develops her inner sense of self. De Beauvoir took long walks through the French countryside as a way of being alone. She was sometimes afraid, but she fully understood the trade-off. Most of the year I live on Long Island, one hundred and fifty miles long with a population larger than that of Ireland. I'm sure I'm a lot safer here than in New York.

In the cabin, next to the bedroom door, is a small bookshelf filled with old books my parents left here. I never go to bed without a book and pull one down entitled *Wilderness Wife*, but, once I lie down, I'm much too tired to read, and turn out the light. Blue curls up on her bed, thick foam covered by a sheepskin, with Ring on an old rug braided with fabric cut from someone's worn-out clothes.

3

The next morning at six thirty, Blue begins a campaign to awaken me. First she paces and scratches herself; then she stares at me. When I finally look her in the eye, she thunks her heavy paw against the bed, so I get up. Today I must go to see my mother.

Ring has let himself out during the night and greets me at the door. The water is cold when I bathe at the dock, but the sun is already warm. The view of the islands and the farther shores is virtually unchanged from the view my parents saw when they first arrived. They would find the addition of only a large white boathouse on Schoolmarm's Point to the north, and a small dock in a cove on Mica Island.

Sputtering from a dead branch at the top of an old sugar maple is a flycatcher called the eastern kingbird. *Tyrannus tyrannus* is his apt Latin name, and my island is his little kingdom. Every year during breeding season this little tyrant sits on the island's highest branch and bickers tiresomely. He will meet head-on any approaching bird he objects to, dueling in midair face to face or following the intruder and attacking it from above. One year a hawk made the mistake of coming near this pair's nest. I was alerted by the kingbirds' explosive squeals and went out in time to see them chasing the hawk, one striking it in the back as it flew. The hawk climbed, turning now and then to defend itself, wing tips spread like fingers. The kingbirds didn't stop but climbed up into hawk-realm, ending up so high I could barely see them before they gave up their chase and descended in great stomach-turning swoops. Then one flew right at me as if to say, "And you too! Back off!" And here I was thinking it was *my* island.

After wrestling a wooden table and some chairs out of the

main room onto the porch, I make breakfast. Blue begins to threaten Ring the minute she smells the bacon, so I tell him to wait outside. They are the best of friends until it's mealtime, when she would try to kill him over food. Ring is used to table scraps, loves bacon, but won't eat fried eggs, so I scramble them. Blue inhales hers while Ring takes his dainty time with a smaller portion on the path outside.

I take my plate to the table at the corner of the porch. Bright, all-yellow warblers—what my mother called wild canaries—are cavorting like butterflies, chasing fat black ants in the birches in front of the cabin. A motorboat passes south of us in a noisy but distant way. The sun's reflection off the gently moving surface of the lake undulates warmly on the shutters, screens, and trees at a heartbeat pace: *ba-boom . . . ba-boom.*

The delicious feeling I have of being alone here is nothing like loneliness. Henry David Thoreau devotes one section of *Walden* entirely to solitude. He stayed alone near Walden Pond in a house smaller than this cabin and wrote:

I am no more lonely than the loon in the pond that laughs so loud. I am no more lonely than a single mullein or dandelion in a pasture, or a bean leaf, or sorrel, or a horse-fly, or a bumblebee.

I discovered my craving for solitude when I realized that I was losing myself. There must be many wives like me who feel their lives were commandeered by the demands of marriage and family. Driving felt empowering the first time I set out alone on the long trip to the lake. The sun seemed brighter and the world full of possibility. I remember loving even the smell of the gasoline as I filled the car's tank on that trip, just part of my freedom ride.

One year, down at the Cedar Haven fishing camp where I'd gone to fill the boat motor's gas tank, I realized that it had been more than a week since I'd spoken to another human being. I'm a social being most of the year, and I love my family, but I'm very fortunate in having not just a room, but an island of my own, where I can go to think my thoughts and lick my wounds. I'm good company for myself, sitting here on my porch or on the dock, surveying all I behold like an eagle in its aerie. I find it both comforting and stimulating.

As I grew up, it was always assumed that I would marry a man who would replace my father and be delighted to assume the out-doorsman role. When I was nineteen, two years after my dad died and the island became mine, I brought my new husband here for a honeymoon and presented it as a fabulous dowry—ta dah! But I was amazed at his level of discomfort once we got to Bobs Lake. I think, being alone on the island with just me, he felt like one of the men who canoed down the river in *Deliverance*—not that he knew how to paddle a canoe.

It had never occurred to me that it could be such a bad fit. I was so young that the obvious hadn't hit me until we arrived. My new husband was nothing like my father. He was no outdoorsman looking to hunt and fish. He was adventuresome in a car and com-petitive on the tennis court, but he was lost in nature. He'd never fished or touched a gun, could barely swim, and was unprepared for the rough and ready with no running water, no indoor toilet, or for the fact that if anything was broken, YOU had to fix it. My friends here were alien to him. He'd walked onto my territory, where I gave orders. He was not going to be at home where he was not in charge.

In retrospect, I realize that he was undoubtedly shocked to find what he'd married into. I'd turned out to be quite different from the college sorority girl he'd known up to then. The result was that I was caught between two men: one who'd taught me to love the whole outdoor wilderness thing and whose spirit pervad-ed my island, and one who hated all that, but to whom I'd sworn my life.

Back on his turf, my husband made sure he was the boss. He would jokingly tell me that I was to consider him "God." Ha-ha. That was a time when women still imposed restrictions on their own freedom and congratulated themselves on their self-imposed conformity to submission. I was no exception, but during the first decade of our marriage, the gears of change were beginning to grind painfully, letting women know it shouldn't be that way.

My husband was twenty-one and headed for graduate school in physics when we married, and he had me convinced about the lofty importance of physics. Even though I understood very little of what he did, it became part of the architecture of my life. It determined where I lived. My friends were "physics wives." I'd find arcane scribbles of equations on the back of my grocery lists. I found myself in one of those marriages in which the woman was supposed to be there for her husband, without any expectation that he be there for her. I was to serve but not be heard.

Maybe that's why I became a writer—to have at least a self-reflective sounding board. I use my journal to sculpt the essence of who I am, recording the thoughts and experiences I have, my reactions to the books I read, as well as moments of unhappiness. I believe writing my complaints there has been a good thing over the years. It's like having someone to talk to, even if the audience for one's own journal writing is hard to define. While it doesn't provide consolation or advice, after howling to the page, it's as though I've been heard in some mysterious way. It helps to defuse some of the pain and anger. And, of course, I bring my joys to my journal as well, so that I can relive them with words.

While solitude for me is seductive, according to my husband there's a need to defend the desire for it. When he tells me that people think me "strange," he says it's because I'm so "confident." This is, of course, his opinion about what others must think. The response I hear from others who know I'm bound for an island is almost always envy for my having a beautiful place for contemplation. In my husband's mind, however, I haven't accomplished anything that could justify what he considers my overconfidence. Nothing, I guess, that gives me the right to be by myself. I told him that I thought I had confidence because I know who I am and what I want and am happy with myself, and that to me he seems *not* to know, to always to be striving to define who he is. He agreed, thinking, I'm sure, that striving is necessary to "get somewhere." Otherwise, you're a "loser."

In 1914 a woman from Maryland chose to spend the winter

here on Bobs Lake *confidently* alone in a small cottage on otherwise uninhabited Mica Island, directly across from my dock. People around here thought that *she* was strange. There seems to be something about islands. In literature the words *island* and *alone* are often bound together, used as symbols of separation, alienation, or even madness, and depicted as home to savages, sorcerers, mutations, willing women, and strange gods. D. H. Lawrence, in the story, "The Man Who Loved Islands," uses increasingly small islands as indicative both figuratively and literally of the withdrawal of "the islander" until he is alone on a rock fearing the approach of man or beast. In other words, s*trange.*

In my lifetime many confident women have set out on solo adventures, setting records for endurance. In 1978, a Polish woman, Krystyna Chojnowska-Liskiewicz, became the first woman to sail around the world alone. It took her 401 days. In 1988, Australian Kay Cottee became the first woman to complete a non-stop circumnavigation of the world, alone at sea for 189 days. In 2005, Dame Ellen MacArthur broke the world record for the fastest solo circumnavigation of the globe, completing the 27,354 nautical-mile trip in seventy-one days, fourteen hours, eighteen minutes and thirty-three seconds. She beat the previous record by one day. And in 2019, Jeanne Socrates, a seventy-seven-year-old British woman, became the oldest person to sail around the world solo and non-stop, *again*, defeating her own record set in 2013. It took her 320 days. Now that's confidence!

Then there is Sarah Marquis, a Swiss woman, who in 2010 began her ten-thousand-mile walk alone at the age of thirty-eight. The National Geographic celebrated her feat by publishing her book, *Wild By Nature: From Siberia to Australia, Three Years Alone in the Wilderness on Foot,* in which she writes: "It was a response to the calling I've got inside me. I want to understand nature and what I'm made of at a deeper level."

I don't mean to put myself in that league, of course, but I do feel an affinity with Cheryl Strayed, who writes in her memoir, *Wild: From Lost to Found on the Pacific Coast Trail,* that she hiked it alone in 1995 because: "Alone had always felt like an actual place to me, as if it weren't a state of being, but rather a room where I could retreat to be what I really was." And I can easily put myself in the place of Alix Kates Shulman who, at age fifty, found peace only by going to live alone on an island off the coast of Maine in a cabin with no plumbing, power, or telephone. She wrote about that in *Drinking the Rain*. If wanting to be alone makes one *strange*, I'm in good company.

To begin with, I should have brought my fiancé here to the island for a trial run, but young people didn't go off together unmarried in those days with little or no contraception. At least not "good girls" like me. We'd dated because I knew and liked his mother, but he and I had utterly different interests, talents, tastes. I loved music, history, and foreign languages. He spoke in the language of mathematics and sports. I fell in love with the idea of him. He had prospects. His father told me that he would need a lot of support in graduate school. I was still a college student, but no one told his son that *I* would need a lot of support.

Our marriage has always felt to me like a competition, but my achievements can't compete with my husband's estimation of success. To him I seem to lack ambition, while in fact all my original ambitions were suppressed by the needs of his career. When we were married, my mother continued to pay my tuition, enabling me to finish my years of undergraduate studies in Latin and history. I'd hoped to go on to a higher degree in classics and received a scholarship for graduate school, but had to make money instead. I worked as a secretary while he finished his PhD. Eventually, two children provided me with a job—but not a profession.

I pursued the life I wanted for myself as much as possible. What was important to me at that time was to play with my children, show them the world, and see it anew through their eyes. I was able to become a good mother and a good musician. They were compatible, but both required hard work. During that time, my daughter dreamed that she and her brother had been kidnapped. Her father went to rescue them, and the kidnapper caught him too. In her dream I rescued all three of them.

Over the years, my husband gained more interest in this summer place, accepting his fate. He bought me a canoe. He added a Sunfish to the fleet. When the roof began to leak, he learned how to be a roofer and put shingles on the cabin.

Still, he would have liked not to vacation in the same place every summer. He always had summer grants to do research with only two weeks free, while I waited impatiently to return to my island. And yet, in order to free him, when I tried bringing the children to the lake without their father, and later came alone, this seemed to him some form of betrayal. At the same time, he never hesitated to spend time away from us on his various ventures. One year, when he was working in Washington D.C., my husband had a dream in which I'd been elected President. We were riding to the inauguration in a limousine, and he was very concerned because he knew I didn't know how to run the country and figured he'd better prepare to help me.

Once my children were more or less grown, I earned a master's degree in English and a job teaching in the same university where my husband was a professor of physics. I became *strangely* confident. Why should self-confidence be strange? Take me or leave me—or I'll leave you. I tried, but somehow I never did. As I swim through life, he's the side of the pool I touch sometimes, confining but safe, a solid element, unlike me.

4

I hear splashing at the shore of Bear Island. An osprey is bathing, just as robins do in a birdbath, burrowing headfirst under the surface, then rising with great wing splashes up onto its back. When it's finished, it takes off, flying toward me over the channel, still shaking water off as it flies, briefly losing balance and height as it does. Then it makes a U-turn to a tiny island, called Goose Island by the Lewises, just off the shore of Bear Island. Hughie's mother had raised geese, and they would fly there to build their nest. The osprey lands on the small island's only remaining tree to stand majestic on its messy nest of sticks.

While I'm washing a few dishes, two pileated woodpeckers are pounding behind the kitchen and bits of an old birch tree fall through its leaves, making the kingbirds sound off. When I was young and my dad heard woodpeckers making holes in his trees, he'd go to get his gun to shoot them. He'd miss and they'd fly away, so luckily, we have no stuffed pileated woodpeckers as décor!

I must leave the lovely lake today, so it's back to the car and the gravel road. Blue would swim after me, so I leave her in the cabin, while Ring will wait outside. From the garage I drive north around Bobs Lake, passing the dam at Bolingbroke and driving on past Crow Lake to the town of Sharbot Lake. An hour after leaving the cabin, I pull in at the Seniors Home, a white clapboard building constructed by linking two houses together. Half the windows, including those of the long dining room on the first floor, afford a close view of the lake.

My mom is sitting in the parlor, not on a couch where I could sit next to her, but in a wheelchair, head drooped, chin to chest, eyes closed. I squat in front of her and speak rather than touch her in order not to startle her. "Hello, Mother," I say, and she raises her head slowly. Then a small smile appears, and she says a soft but pleasant "Hello." She has no idea who I am.

Eleven years ago, after my mother had nursed her second husband through the bone cancer that ended his life, I realized that dementia was making it impossible for her to live alone in her apartment at Leisure World in Southern California. If I called and asked her how she was, she'd say, "Well, my forgetter is working well." Her friends told me that she never spoke of me, that it was as though I didn't exist, though I called her often from New York, checking on her, reminding her of standing appointments. She had a prescription plan but didn't know it, and wouldn't remember what to take or when to take it. She continued to drive but would become lost.

When she suffered an angina attack in a parking lot and was taken to the hospital, she didn't ask that anyone be notified, and for days I couldn't reach her. I called her neighbor to inquire. She didn't know either but finally located Dorothea for me.

I flew to California and found that my mother had been preyed upon. Even within a gated community she hadn't been safe. She'd been sold seventeen insurance policies, most of them duplicates, several from the same company. Someone came every six months to take down her drapes to "clean" them for $500. She received almost daily phone calls asking for money for political donations. A personalized letter would come in the mail reminding her that she'd pledged, and she'd write a nice check for something like "Ollie North's birthday."

She had always insisted that she never wanted to be a burden to me, but rather than find a nursing home for her where she was living, three thousand miles away, I was able to persuade her to move east to my home on Long Island where I could care for her. She seemed frail, and I thought she wouldn't live much longer. As the movers loaded some of her things onto the moving van, she sat and played her beloved piano for the last time. I cried. She didn't. She was always stoical.

At our home in New York, I improved her diet and put nitroglycerine patches on her every day until the angina disappeared. She was cheerful and grateful, entertaining herself well while I was at work with simple word puzzles, solitaire, jigsaw puzzles, books, and TV. In the evening she would often play me a concert on my piano while I cooked dinner, but gradually her ability to do these things fell away. Blue became her beloved close companion, a friend who didn't care about her confusions.

I assumed responsibility for all her affairs. My son, James, who has always had great empathy with the elderly, must have seemed a better friend to her than I was. I was the one who had to tell her what to do. Then, after more than six years with us, having lost nearly all her physical and mental abilities, she needed more care than I could give. Years before, Ervin's wife, June, had given me the idea of having her stay in the Seniors Home in Sharbot Lake while I was on the island each summer. That had gone well, until after six years she thought I was kidnapping her when I picked her up for the return trip to New York, crying and angry with me all the way.

Dementia makes change terrifying. The following year, the Seniors Home seemed a natural place in which to relocate her permanently, homey, and comfortably furnished with antiques. I began driving back and forth once a month from Long Island to see her. My oldest friend, Ervin's sister Joan, lives nearby and became my mother's advocate when I wasn't here, stopping every day on her way home after work at the Sears outlet.

* * *

In spite of her sweater and the warmth in the room, my mother feels cold. Tucking her lap robe more tightly about her, I realize that it's warmer outside in the sun than here in the parlor. I fetch a hat for her from her room, unlock the wheels on her chair and take her out for a little tour of the garden, but it isn't long before she becomes anxious, not knowing where we are or who I am.

"We'd better go back," she says. "I'll miss the bus. They'll all wonder where I am."

There's no arguing with her, so I take her back to the familiar parlor and go upstairs to check in with the director of the Home. She tells me that my mother's appetite is waning. At lunch I try to feed her, but she'll take only a little apple sauce and mashed potato. She used to love food, but gradually her mental disorder has poisoned all her pleasures.

The marriage of my parents was an unlikely union. She was the daughter of Baptist missionaries who'd given her the name *Dorothea*, "gift of God." She'd been born only a few months before her parents, Sam and Minnie Bawden, left for India, taking her and her four-year-old brother along with them. Her father was an "industrial" missionary, there to create better economic conditions among *the untouchables*, the lowest caste in India. They took responsibility for prisoners of the Raj, tribal people in the hills of southern India who stole from anyone who ventured onto their lands, sometimes cutting the nose or earlobes of women for their jewels. Police would capture the men and make them work in mines.

My grandparents' idea was to give these people a chance to enter a different way of life and to include their entire families, with health care and school for the children. The Raj provided about three thousand acres of land south of Madras at Kavali. Sam supervised the men in roadmaking, building houses and bridges, quarrying, draining of the land for farming, digging wells, and irrigation. He learned their language, Telegu, in order to preach the gospel and translate the Bible. Minnie oversaw the teaching of women and children and ran a health clinic.

Every seven years the Bawdens had a furlough of one year that allowed them to return to the United States. It had been difficult to keep my mother healthy and safe in Southern India during those first seven years. Minnie breast-fed her for two years to protect her, but before they left India on their first furlough, Dorothea had contracted malaria, diphtheria, and typhoid. She'd become infected by head lice, treated by soaking her head in kerosene overnight. The feet of their beds were set into cans of kerosene to discourage sleeping with scorpions and poisonous snakes. So, when they returned to the United States on furlough, the Bawdens left their two children to be raised in the Fanny Doane Home for Missionary Children in Granville, Ohio.

When her parents were to depart for India, leaving her behind, Dorothea was told by her maternal grandmother that she must not cry because it would make it harder for her mother. Everyone else in the family cried, but she did not. She remembered standing on the train platform, her father weeping, her mother sobbing, her brother in tears. She held her grandfather's hand and watched tears stream from his eyes into his beard, fascinated, because up to then she hadn't thought men ever cried. Her mother said afterward that it would have been better if she *had* cried.

My dad, Philip Eichenlaub, had also been semi-orphaned. I think he would have been a different person if his Irish mother hadn't died when he was three. His father, needing help in raising two young children, called upon *his* mother to live with him and take care of them. She was a bitter woman, and Phil was always in trouble at home, slipping out of the house at night from his bedroom window and down a tree. And yet, according to his sister, he was the nuns' darling in Catholic school, high-spirited, handsome, athletic, a voracious reader, and a highly praised cartoonist. He went on to study at the Cleveland School of Art and later worked as sports editor for his hometown newspaper in Ohio, *The Akron Beacon Journal*. When America entered the First World War, he became a soldier and was sent to Camp Sherman in Chillicothe, Ohio, for military training. A young woman from Akron followed him there and, shortly before he sailed for France, he married her.

When he returned from the war, my dad became a chiropractor and eventually set up a practice in Kent. He and his wife had a daughter. His career was to be a success, but the marriage ended very badly. When he found his wife with another man, he punched her and broke her jaw. I didn't know my father's first daughter well, but once, in a letter, I apologized for never having asked her about her mother. Her reply was: "My mother was a slut." She said of our father, "He demanded perfection of everyone but himself," but despite her list of his cruelties, she was determined to love and defend him.

When he divorced, Phil was not only excommunicated by the Catholic Church, his father and sister excommunicated him too, refusing to meet Dorothea when he remarried. At his father's death they remained unreconciled. I first met his sister the day my dad died, when she came to the hospital wanting to make sure that he was given the last rites. My father refused.

I've never understood how my parents happened to meet and fall in love. They never talked about it, and it's too late to ask.

Dorothea   Phil

5

Before I return to Bobs Lake where there is no cell phone service, I leave a message for my husband on our home phone, saying I've arrived here safely.

Back at the cabin, Blue leads the way to the kitchen. I open two cans of tuna, one for me and one for them, mixing theirs with dry dog food. The rest of the year Blue is fed canned dog food once a day. What she loves most about being here, I believe, is that here I cater to our fresh-air appetites twice a day. Ring slowly and carefully eats half of what I give him, then turns down the path. A few days of running and swimming will make him a hungry dog too, but fundamentally he, unlike Blue, eats to live rather than living to eat. For me, one of the pleasures of being alone is eating when and what I feel like and having almost no dishes to wash. I arrange my tuna on a plate with sliced tomato, cold canned green beans, radishes, and some mayonnaise.

The land lies mellow in the evening, the sky and lake competing to see which can be bluer. I head down the path to the boathouse. The last time my father was here, he was dying. He walked me around the island and cabin, pointing out things that would need to be done, teaching me how to do them, preparing this teenager as well as he could to take over as the islander, which I felt at the time meant being like him. I did not aspire to be anything like my mother.

At that time, the back of our island still had a protective sand beach, and we could walk around on it. During the last years of my dad's life, waves from increasing boat traffic were eroding the shores along the front of the island. That drove my dad to spend a few years finding large rocks to place along the waterline, which my mother was sure had contributed to his deteriorating health. It wasn't unusual for our lake to rise above its designated maximum height, especially in spring after the melt-off of snow, but the dam at the north end of the lake at Bolingbroke had recently been "rebuilt," raising the standard water level above its former height.

Before this lake was first dammed in 1821, its level was fifteen to eighteen feet lower than it is now, and where I'm standing was not yet an island. Each time the dam has been enlarged over the years, more forest land has been drowned and the island grows smaller. Our beach is long gone now. The soft woodland soil makes for a rich wildlife habitat, but waves from boat traffic and storms drive the water deep into the roots of trees and shrubs, causing them to lose their footing. I estimate that in my lifetime I've lost a quarter of what the island was when I was born.

The year a spring thaw brought water up to a back corner of our cabin, I began my reclamation project. For more than twenty summers I've come to work on my rock wall, carrying in sixty-six-pound bags of concrete mix, clearing a trench, fitting large rocks into it as a base for others, hauling water and mixing the cement by hand in an old dish pan, working in the underbrush with mosquitoes and flies, day after day, until I can barely move. Gloves are too big for small crevices and heavy with my hands in and out of water, so I lay cement with my hands bare until my skin is cut and raw. Often rocks slip and smash my fingers. At night I have trouble sleeping because my swollen hands go numb and my body aches.

All of this long ago prompted my husband to shake his head and insist that my vacations consisted of work which, had I been sentenced to do it, would be considered cruel and unusual. He almost convinced me to stop trying to fight Mother Nature, particularly when I began to feel some real funny clicks in my spine every time I lifted a bag of sand, soil, or cement mix into the trunk of my car, out of the trunk and down to the boat, then out of the boat and up across the catwalk to the wheelbarrow, then across the island and out to the worksite.

As the years went on, back in New York, I would decide not to work on the wall. But once on the island, I couldn't resist the compulsion. When a section was complete, perhaps ten or twelve feet, I'd build a supporting shelf toward the lake with rock, pebbles, and sand, with great rocks too big to lift rolled in from offshore to hold the shelf in. My son, James, and some of his friends provided welcome strength. Lastly, I'd fill behind the wall with leaves, branches, and bags of soil. In some places I have double walls, one inside another, with double terracing. There is nothing I can do about the ends of the island, where we're losing ground rapidly, but my goal was to save the cabin while keeping the look as natural as possible.

I wasn't consciously trying to *be* my father, but I knew what I was doing—holding these cabin logs sacred like ancestors' bones. During two years in my early married life, when we lived in California and I was unable to come here, I would have nightmares in which the cabin was threatened by fire or flood. In a sense, then, what was happening to the island was my worst nightmare come true. It was as though I, myself, were under siege.

I haven't lost my compulsion, but I have lost some of my capacity for work, and nowadays it takes me days, if not weeks, to face up to it. There's talk of "improving" the dam once again. Someday there will be just a log cabin surrounded by water.

I pass the place where I anchored the first stretch of my rock wall at a slightly raised piece of ground where we used to have a woodpile. The wood has since rotted into soil, but two years before he died, it was on that woodpile that my dad set up a small piece of white birch bark, put the .22 rifle into my hands, and taught me how to hold and aim the gun and squeeze the trigger. In the process of doing this, he fired a shot, saying he'd hit the birch bark tab. When I shot, he told me I'd missed. We walked to the target and found two small holes in it. If he hit it, I hit it.

In the boathouse, little brown bats have been roosting under the roof, and their droppings decorate the bottom of the canoe. I find them dead sometimes, their tiny bodies—smaller than a mouse—shriveled, but their long wings still like supple leather. I slide the canoe through the double doors, turn it over, throw in a paddle, and lift it carefully over some rocks and into the lake. From the back dock behind the cabin, Ring springs lightly into the center of it. I circle our island, inspecting the shoreline closely, Blue swimming alongside. The wall I've been building is crumbling in places. Where there is no wall, beavers fell trees and strip shrubs. I see two young trees lying with their tops in the lake.

When I enter the channel, Blue swims on without me, heading for Wilson's Bay. Seeing Blue leaving us, Ring gives a huffy sigh and looks the other way. I laugh at him and his ears soften toward me. During his first few years vacationing with me, Ring wouldn't swim. He was reluctant even to get a foot wet, and on excursions I had to deposit his highness on dry land, finding a place where I could bring the boat in far enough for him, sometimes getting my own feet wet in the process. Finally, a day came when he decided to follow Blue into the water and became free to come and go from the farm. However, he's no champion swimmer, not having big webbed feet like Blue's, and he always prefers to be chauffeured.

I call Blue so that she'll stay with me. Her black head won't be visible from speeding boats. Giving up her own purpose for the promise of mine, she follows, and we head for the shallow pass between Bear and Mica Islands, which separate our inner channel from the larger one beyond. There's only a slight breeze, but I turn into it along the far side of Mica Island so that as I circle around it, the wind will be behind me heading home. Blue finds a place to climb ashore and disappears to explore.

In the main channel, Ring and I pass the old cottage high on a rocky cliff where, in 1914, the writer Laura Lee Davidson, a grand-niece of the Civil War general Robert E. Lee, spent a winter alone. It's not a place easily visited, the steep path up to it hidden in the bush. She wrote a book about her experience entitled *A Winter of Content.* Laura Lee wrote two more books about this lake, all long out of print. For years I looked for them in vain, until the internet made it possible to dredge up copies and I could pore over her words about Bobs Lake, which she ponderously renamed "The Lake of Many Islands."

Of course, people thought Laura Lee was strange. She doesn't explain why she, a schoolteacher from Baltimore, Maryland, chose to winter alone on an island in such extreme conditions—with cold occasionally as low as 35°F below zero, snow up to her arm-pits and no way to call for help—just that she needed "rest." She says she was warned by her family:

"'You'll freeze your nose and ears off,' mourned a reassuring aunt.

'You'll break a leg and lie for days before anyone knows you are hurt,' said Cousin John.

'You'll be snowed in and no one will find you until spring,' said Brother Henry.

'You are a city woman and not strong. What do you know of a pioneer's life? It is the most foolish plan we ever heard of,' chorused all."

And yet, near the end of *A Winter of Content,* she says it has brought her "health." Not that she wasn't terrified her first few nights alone. She slept with a pistol next to her pillow, though more afraid, she says, of the gun than of anything she'd be tempted to use it against.

I can understand Laura Lee's need to prove something to herself by staying alone on a wilderness island, but winter alone here would be too daunting for me. Whatever it was that sent her running from Baltimore, she had determination enough to strug-gle without help when she hurt her foot and had to carry a chair around everywhere to lean or kneel on. She nearly burned the little cottage down through her inexperience with wood stoves. In return, she gained a universe, describing each thing in her new world as a way of seeing it, becoming one with it all, gaining an intimate relationship with this place as though it were an organism that could embrace her as she embraced it.

Mica Island is a fortress compared to mine, larger, higher, and with rock cliff ramparts around much of it. There is a beaver feeding station on a low part of the shore where my shrubs and branches end up, as though I'm paying liege. As the world raged into the First World War, Laura Lee did not return to Bobs Lake for three years. When she did, she spent all her summers here, at first on Mica Island with the friend who owned the place, visits described in her book, *Isles of Eden*. Later, she built a log house of her own on the point of the peninsula that forms the other side of Lewis Bay, north of me. Because she taught school in the States, her place became known by the locals as Schoolmarm's Point.

In 1924, at a time when there were only two motors for propelling boats on this part of Bobs Lake, Laura Lee wrote: *"Alas, we fear . . . that, all too soon, our lake will become known to campers. . . . Then motorboats will go snorting about, spoiling the fishing and frightening the herons and loons away to wilder waters, and our silence will be broken by boat-loads of "sports" yelling and singing in the twilight and moonlight."* While her first two books refer to her experiences here in 1914 and 1918, they were published a decade later, during the time when the wealthy Wilsons were developing the peninsula directly west of Mica Island. She makes no reference to them, but perhaps they were the cause for her concern about noisy summer visitors and their impact upon the wildlife here.

Laura Lee wasn't widely admired on the lake. Her strict piety and Southern parochialism made her a bad fit with those who lived in this pioneer land. People were kind to her that winter. She could buy bread and milk from a farm family on Timmerman's island, and some gave her venison and maple syrup, cut and carried her firewood, brought her mail and transported her to town when she needed to go. Fishermen sometimes shared their catch with her, but if it included bullheads, she would throw those in the lake rather than eat them.

What she wrote about people was often unflattering, and many resented her judgments. In a letter written late in her life, she admitted to Dr. Goodfellow of Westport that she'd changed the names of people she'd written about, and even the name of the lake, so that she could not be held liable for misinformation. This, she thought, freed her to say whatever she liked, and she was condescending enough to believe that the residents of the lake would never discover and read her books. She was wrong. They did and had less reason to befriend her afterward.

Near the end of her life, Laura Lee agreed to sell to my dad the place she'd built on Schoolmarm's Point. He brought cash to pay her, but at the last minute she raised the price and he backed out. I was five years old then and remember being relieved that we would not be leaving our island and cabin.

6

Ring and I return down the inner channel and meet Blue swimming home. The lake is calm now, the surface like glass, inviting you to look at all that lies below. You could drop a worm on a hook and watch the small fish poke at it and the larger ones ignore it.

The long June evening purrs along like a love song. Everything is as it should be, here where nothing happens . . . and everything happens. The dogs lie on the island while I sit on the dock and watch as attentively as I might watch TV. Each evening is different and must be studied. The islands across the channel from me seem to float on the surface of the lake, lit up obliquely by the yielding sun. Up in the pass a herring gull floats, looking this way and that, just as I am.

For a while a fisherman named Carl tries to tempt bass on the shoal by Bear Island. He has a small place on the southern peninsula and comes each summer to fish. As the sun retreats, it paints the clouds, which reflect pink and violet on the surface of the channel where little water skaters zigzag crazily and fish are flopping to feed on them. A muskrat swims to the dock without noticing that I'm there and floats, not moving. When I rise to see its tail to be sure it's a muskrat and not a beaver, it gives a little shriek and dives. Carl gives up and motors away, and near me a large turtle pokes her fist-sized head up in the channel to breathe for a few seconds before dipping below once again.

Across the bay on Schoolmarm's point is Laura Lee's cabin on higher ground, protected by natural rock outcroppings. Would my memories of my long dead dad remain as indelible for me if we had moved there? She looked down on the lake, whereas, by being nearly *in* the lake, my island makes me feel as one with this wild place, not an observer from above. I can't imagine loving that place, but at least I would not have had to lay down rock bones in its soil.

As the sun sinks below the western hill, the great blue heron flies low along the edges of Bear and Mica Islands, headed south toward the marsh and his roost. Mosquitos begin to hum and the dogs suggest we go inside, but it's hard to leave. The moon, all made up for evening, is becoming full of herself, seeking center stage. I see her and she sees me. She too is alone. A loon passes close to me with a soft hooting call and makes ripples when it dives. Only when a slight breeze comes up do I take us three into the house. If I could have but one hour in life, this one would suffice.

In the cabin Blue goes directly to her bed, turning herself three times before she falls, but Ring stays in the living room, waiting until I settle on the futon with the old book I found on the shelf. He joins me there and pushes his head under my arm. When I tire of hugging him, he cuddles himself as close to me as he can.

My mother has written my dad's name inside the cover of this book, *Wilderness Wife: The Story of a Home in the North Woods*, by Kathrene Pinkerton, published in 1939. Mrs. Pinkerton's book tells how she and her husband willingly gave up their urban careers in the States to set up housekeeping in the wilderness of Canada, somewhere between Lake Superior and Hudson Bay. Mrs. Pinkerton isn't clear about where, but it was far enough north that there was danger of "frost in eleven, sometimes twelve months of the year."

The reason for their move was a doctor's summary ultimatum that made her husband quit his job as a newspaperman in Wisconsin for "a new job, daytime hours, fresh air and exercise, a different routine of living. It was not a prescription we could fill at the drugstore on the corner." That is as far as she goes in explaining his ailment. Her husband's solution sounds like bad medicine to me, and I hope I wouldn't have fallen for it. Kathrene, who had a degree in sociology from the University of Wisconsin, gave up a position as field secretary for the Wisconsin Anti-Tuberculosis Association.

With remarkable intrepidity for a man so threatened, Robert Pinkerton took his wife into the wild with nearly nothing. They got off a train in a "raw hamlet . . . the one railroad stop in two hundred miles that had both store and post office," only $8 in their pockets. From there they set out deep into the wilderness in a canoe, with only a few tools and weapons, looking for a place to build miles from anyone else. She jovially describes the agony of kneeling and paddling a canoe around for days, looking for a site. No one could accuse Kathrene of complaining.

"A new job?" she writes. "We would try writing fiction. Rent and groceries? The wilderness would supply all of the first and most of the second."

I wish I could ask my mother what she thought of this book, but she wouldn't know what I was talking about now. I'm at home here in my island paradise, but sadly home is not with my mother. She is alone in the terrifying wilderness of dementia, helpless, needing to be fed and lifted, diaper changed, bathed, crying out when people come to haul her up to attend to her. It's not that anyone is cruel, but her body objects to these required tasks, joints sore, her thin skin fragile and easily torn or bruised, her feet swollen, her legs and arms always cold.

I wonder why we try to live long lives if old age can have such humiliating, painful and pointless things in store. I've never understood those who feel that there is some plan for things like this, that a plotting mind with infinite wisdom would arrange to give my mother half again as much life as my father but deprive her of the brain to use it for anything.

My feelings about my parents, particularly my father, are complicated. In most ways I had a normal mid-century, middle-class, Midwestern upbringing, but not one dulled by perfection. My parents loved each other, were dependable in their responsibility toward me, and gave me rich experiences of life, but I remember being surprised, once, when my mother told me that my dad loved me very much.

His alcoholism was something that affected us all. Both of my parents tried to protect me from it, but all children of alcoholics are victims to differing degrees. As I grew up, I became aware of his occasional tendency to relieve his pressures through drink, and of the stigma attached to this. Addiction, in a small town in Ohio at a time when there was little or no social drinking, was judged as a moral failing. Particularly as a teenager, I was afraid he would betray us.

Because of his profession, my dad tried never to drink, and he succeeded most of the time, but when things became too much for him, as things cost more and he felt he couldn't charge his patients more, with a child approaching college and no social security for self-employed professionals in those days, no retirement packages, he would disappear for a couple of hours. Our lives depended upon his willpower. I can clearly remember my mother's concern one evening when patients began to build up in the waiting room and she realized my dad wasn't in the house. Eventually she turned away his patients and went out to find him. On nights like that, she said that, after I went to bed, she'd sit up late, knitting or doing something with her hands, while he talked on and on.

I'd always known that my father was a good person, open-minded and big-hearted, believing in social fairness for the little guy. Before marrying my mother, my dad had under his wing a man named Harold, in those days referred to as a "moron" or "half-wit," who had no one to care for him and no means of employment. My dad took him in, fed him, and gave him work that provided him with a sense of purpose.

Chiropractic was a crusade in the 1920s and 30s, and my dad, for all his rough edges, was a missionary in his own right, flaunting the banner of chiropractic against the strong anti-chiropractic lobby, the American Medical Association. When he began his practice, he charged patients one dollar for an "adjustment" and ten dollars for an X-ray: Depression rates. When he died thirty-five years later, he was still charging the same amount, refusing to burden his patients more. For him it was a social cause.

We weren't badly off because he had so many patients. He did not make appointments, but each evening our living room would fill with people seeking help from him. After high school games, I'd often come home in my band uniform to find one of the football players in our living room, waiting for my father to straighten him out. Still, as my college years approached, he'd pace the rubber runner in the hall from the waiting room to his office at the end of a day, counting the dollar bills in his worn black wallet, frowning with concentrated worry, pacing back the other way, moving his lips as he counted again. After his death, I found that he'd saved enough money to put me through college. It's in this way that my father was strong. It's in this way that I wanted to be like him.

While I was afraid of him when I was young, I ended up with a great deal of respect for him. When I wrote for my high school newspaper, I'd listen to him talk at the supper table, then go upstairs and write good copy. He didn't tell me what he thought when the paper's best editorial of the year was declared to be one that reflected his opinion about the competition between the United States and the Soviet Union in the field of science education. I've long missed his quick wit, his intellect, his healing hands. He was the only doctor I ever saw until he was dead.

But my mother has become two women for me. One married my dad, had me, and loved us both. After my father died, she moved to Orange County in southern California, married a very different man, a puritanical teetotaler, and, like a chameleon, my mom changed her color. I was glad that she had found a companion, but her new husband seemed to represent everything my father had opposed, and I couldn't understand how my mom could love the second man after loving the first. It seemed a betrayal of all she had been when she raised me.

She'd told her friends that she would remarry only if she found a millionaire, and she did. She married a rich widower. They started each day by discussing the fluctuations in his stock holdings. When she visited us, she would tell us that he thought the Saudi Arabians had the right idea in chopping off the hands of thieves. In the early 1980s, she warned my friends that the Soviet flag would soon be flying over the White House. Her husband told me that national forests should be sold for timber.

Of course, as a role model, my dad was terrible. One summer when I was a kid, after hearing my mother trying to stop him from swearing within my hearing, I challenged my dad to give me a nickel every time I heard him use a bad word. Candy bars sold for five cents in those days. At first, he had to pay out a bit now and then. It led to parsing such issues as whether "goddamn" and "son-of-a-bitch" are two separate curses when uttered together and therefore worth ten cents. Then came a day when I was standing on the dock and my parents were in the boat preparing to go down to the fishing camp for gas. They'd floated out into the channel, but my dad was still standing up when my mother, her back to him, pulled the starter rope. The motor had been left in forward gear, causing the boat to surge forward. He fell back onto a seat clutching the side of the boat. I was sure I was going to be rich as I counted up by fives until they were halfway to the pass and I couldn't hear him anymore. But he'd had enough of the game. He refused to pay and ended the deal.

He wasn't partial to the potty words. I never heard him say "shit," "crap," or "piss." He would "take a leak." His profanity preferences seemed aimed more toward his rejected Catholicism, usually involving J.C. When I was a teenager sleeping late in my bedroom one morning, he added to my vocabulary. Clearly not realizing I was there, he banged around, looking for something in the gun room next door, until, in frustration, he enunciated loudly: "Well, cock-sucking fucking Jesus Christ!" I doubt that any of my friends' parents had accomplished such virtuosity.

I've always wondered how my dad managed to hold his tongue for ten days when he brought two ministers with him to the island to fish one spring. Joe Henderson preached at the Methodist Church where my mother sang, and he brought along a friend, Reverend Young, probably hoping to outnumber the heathen. The day they left to return home was stormy. Hughie was assigned to transport the two men of the cloth across the lake in his boat, while my dad took all the gear. The ministers prayed all the way across the lake. Phil was told to come to church the next week to hear the sermon about how Hughie, with God's help, delivered them from the storm. Phil had a lot of fun teasing Hughie about that. And a few years later he brought the Reverend Fred Thomas, minister of the Union Baptist Church in Kent, a friend of my grandmother's. None of them returned for a second time.

The Reverend Fred Thomas and Phil

7

I wake up to the sound of Ervin's cattle bawling lazily across the bay where they've come down to drink. Through the window I watch seven young ducklings following their momma behind the island, all moving as one large duck atom, no sound. Song sparrows have hatchlings in a tree cavity by the path to the outhouse. The parents have been too busy to sit on a branch and sing their bright, intricate songs, but raucous baby cheeps erupt whenever I approach the nest. I'm living in a nursery. And a female ruby-throated hummingbird has begun to build her nest in the cedars near the porch, the tiny roar of her wings describing each take-off and return. Where her mate's throat would be ruby red, hers is white, but her feathers are sparkly metallic green on her back, head, and wings. No sign of him. I watch through the screen with binoculars as she brings plant fluff and the gauze of spider webs to form a silky white nest fastened onto the side of a branch.

To get lake water running to the old cast iron sink, I run the flexible pipe to the edge of the bluff at the front of the island and drop the intake valve into the lake below, weighted down with a rock. In the boathouse I find my dad's hammer and just the right wrench to loosen the valves on the small pump. It takes pail after pail of lake water to prime the pump outside the kitchen until the motor can draw steadily from the lake.

With running water at last, I begin cleaning the cabin in earnest, sweeping the floors and shaking the rugs. Bordering two sides of the main room is the wide screened porch with the enclosed kitchen at one end. On a third side are two bedrooms, one small, the other, which my dad added on for me, somewhat larger. Bark was left on all the logs, inside and out, and they were chinked with cement whitened with lime.

I tie the clothesline between two trees and hang pillows and a blanket to air, listening to the radio as I come and go. Radio programming in Canada has always linked a small population in a vast land, where not everyone had television or other forms of reception, and it often provides a national forum on big issues, interesting to me because of its outside perspective on the United States. I also learn about aboriginal points of view and their struggles. One Dene man is quoted as saying that the young of his people had drifted away from the land, from the old ways, "like a ship without a halter," an interesting mixed metaphor. In addition, I enjoy a wide variety of music, book reviews, drama, and light entertainment.

Today the FM 108 station is enjoying hours of invited fish stories. They announce the subject and people call in, men and women, highfliers and low, funny and serious, good story tellers and lousy. No competition, just gentle reminiscence and humor. Listening to them makes the work easier.

While I'm here in the cabin, I feel I'm with both of my parents. My dad's presence is everywhere, even in the kitchen, where I find recipes scrawled in his distinctive hand. He did the cooking during the spring and fall when he brought men to the cabin to hunt. He would plan for them in Kent and bring the needed ingredients to the island. For meat they'd eat what they could catch or kill, depending upon their luck, but he always had a backup, like a slice of ham, baked beans, or reconstituted dried beef in milk gravy. His desserts were ambitious, each day something new: Epicurean apricots; apple, lemon, or pumpkin pie; white or chocolate cake; upside-down cake; everything made from scratch. No frozen pie crusts or mixes or packaged frostings in those days. He would assign cleanup to others.

My mother's apron still hangs behind the kitchen door and on the shelves are the dogwood-patterned dishes she loved. While I was a child and we were here in summer, she did the cooking and managed, without electricity, to produce hearty meals from this small kitchen, using the kerosene stove and an icebox cooled with

chunks of ice that Hughie Lewis had cut from the lake in winter
and stored in sawdust in the Wilsons' icehouse—the only building
that had survived the fire on the peninsula. Hydroelectricity came
to the cabin in the 1950s through a submarine cable, and my work
is much easier than theirs was in those early days.

After the First World War, many people seemed to long to get
away from so-called "civilization." That must have been part of
the motivation for my dad when he bought the island from Mrs.
Wilson in the 1930s. Fishing camps were popular, and Bobs Lake
had several of them. Of course, the vacation style of those times,
the popularity of camping out in the woods, was for most people
playing at living differently. It's fun to dress down and get dirty and
boil water for washing dishes and even to use the outhouse—as
long as it's above sixty degrees. I like the fact that there's no TV
here, no car outside the door, and no telephone, but I appreciate
no longer having to clean the glass chimneys on oil lamps, haul
buckets of water from the lake, or bring in ice for an icebox. I
want to have my cake and eat it too.

Living here has always been, for us, a reminder that it's an
insects' world. This old log cabin isn't sealed perfectly and is wel-
coming to small creatures. Mosquitos sometimes go to bed with
me and sing me annoying lullabies. The daddy longlegs bounce
around the floor and occasionally walk over a sleeping dog's nose,
causing a big snort and shake. I actually enjoy living with them,
such harmless creatures. And I welcome the pretty black and yellow wasps, called mud daubers, who all my life have built their clay
constructions on the high ceiling of the main room. They prey
upon the spiders. When I arrive here each year, a few of these mud
daubers bump against the inside of the porch screens, unable to
find their customary exits, confused by the sudden amplitude of
light until they figure it out. They're harmless and allow me to capture them in a glass and release them through the door. Bumble
bees seldom appear inside the cabin, although I was repulsed one
year when I put my hand into an old bathrobe pocket and found
it full of their waxy, slimy green brood cells. I had to throw that
bathrobe away.

Outside are the fierce yellow jackets, who sometimes build their paper nests between the window screens and the outside shutters. Because my husband is allergic to stings, if he's here, it's my job to open the shutters on our arrival. If I find a yellow jacket nest, which is not uncommon, I have to put on my armor—two pairs of long pants tucked into boots, long sleeves tucked into gloves, a hat and scarf and swim goggles—and find the bottle of flying insect spray. A whole air force of them will try to overcome me, seeking openings in my clothing, clustering on the goggles, seeking my eyes. That's nightmare stuff. I spray their nest so they'll go elsewhere, and then run.

The last thing I do before I put on a bathing suit and carry a deck chair to the dock is to find Marian Wilson's wind chimes, dating from the 1920s, and I stand on a stool to hang them from a joist on the porch. The glass pieces collide to produce a high tinkling sound, like ethereal laughter.

I wade into the water and let out the front dock, testing the chains and lengthening the reach so that it will float as the lake level goes down. My two docks are like floating rooms, the front one with morning and afternoon light, the newer one behind the cabin lit in the evening. This old one in front is growing closer each year to being part of the island itself. Exposure has softened the planking on top of the logs, warping it, making it slippery in places. The end of each board looks chewed. Leaves, cedar needles, and dung have filled the crevices with enough soft organic matter to support bright red and soft sage-green lichens; bristly dark green mosses with hairy spikes; velvety smooth moss the color of a billiard table; and even grasses and tree seedlings. Here and there are broken pieces of clam and snail shells and dried fish bones, evidence of the muskrats, raccoons, herons, and gulls that use the dock as a platform while I'm not here. It floats so low that the ducks and mergansers, even their little ones, hop up onto it to look around and preen.

I swim out into the lake and Blue leaps in to join me. When I return and pull myself out, hoping to sit in the deck chair in the sun and read, Blue brings me a stick. I can't ignore her, so I indulge her by throwing the stick far out over the water. She leaps off the dock, head held high, and fetches it, not back to the dock but to the edge of the island, clambering slowly up over the rocks. Ring waits there to take the stick away from her. She's less agile than Ring on her land legs.

Blue was a Christmas present I gave to my son James. On Long Island, when she was six months old, a car went over Blue and broke two of her legs. My mother told James that she'd pay the orthopedic veterinary bills, so Blue went on with her life, chasing squirrels in the yard as though it hadn't happened, running with her right foreleg and left hindleg in heavy casts. Even though the skin underneath was chafed raw, she seemed oblivious to pain. When the casts came off, swimming here in the lake was good physical therapy, and she seemed as good as new.

While my mother lived with us, Blue was her best friend. Someone who didn't notice her memory loss. During her first full year in the Home in Sharbot Lake, my mother still remembered Blue, and became desperate to find her each time she heard a dog bark. The staff put a bracelet on her to set off an alarm if she went out. Yet if I brought Blue to visit her, she greeted her out of a love for all dogs, but had no recollection of this one in particular. Friends become strangers in Dorothea's world.

Sometimes I think she married my dad for his two big English setters, Chief and Bones, whose tails would thump the floor when she entered a room. She'd never been allowed to own a dog. She'd tell about wanting as a child to take care of a mongrel she saw wandering in India and being told no, and there was no pet for her in the missionary children's home in Ohio, so from the moment she married my dad, there was always a dog. They seemed to offer her a portal to love and affection. Before my dad died, I never saw my mother cry, except when one of our dogs died.

My mother stunned me once by telling me that she took people at face value, never trying to know them below the surface. When I think back about it, it's true that, while she was liked and admired and seemed to like others, she had no best friends or confidantes. On the other hand, she was devoted to my father and couldn't have been a better mother to me.

While Dorothea was growing up, she'd belonged to the large community offered by Granville's missionary children's home and Baptist church, where she felt safe, even special, but they weren't family. Her parents' occupation was highly regarded by everyone she knew, excusing them from dereliction as parents. To my knowledge, she never questioned their commitment to their cause. She seems to have been firmly convinced that their putting God ahead of her was the right and good thing to do. During her institutional childhood, she'd learned to present an ostensibly cheerful acceptance of her role no matter what the circumstances. While the family managed to maintain strong ties through letters, what my mother craved, it seemed, was the intimacy of family life, something she'd had again with us, dog and all, when I moved her to our home on Long Island.

Dorothea at 92

I drowse in my deck chair listening to a congress of crows disputing some issue on the peninsula. Here on the lake, I'm audience for a vast drama that I seldom understand. I don't know what birds are saying, but I always believe what they're saying is true, except for crows. With crows I'm not so sure.

I lie there, book open on my chest, dogs carpeting the shady path to the cabin, when something causes me to open my eyes. A black water snake, about four feet long, is stretched out alongside me at the end of the dock. There are no venomous snakes here.

I often see these snakes hunting along the shore for frogs, sala-manders, crayfish, or minnows. I've never been afraid of them, although they always bring me up short when I lift the side of a turned-over boat and find myself standing next to a big one. It scares the snake too, and it hurries away, but now, together for a while, this one and I both lie perfectly still. I'm honored to share with her this moment in the sun.

Then a fast boat turns into our channel, Blue comes to life and barks at it, waves dash, and Snake is gone. I didn't see her go.

8

As the June days progress, Ms. Hummingbird works on her nest, fluttering her body into the material to shape it. She leaves frequently to zoom over the water to the hummingbird feeder that Ervin's daughter, Julie, put up at their house, and for a while I'll hear no more purr of wings.

I've been at home with the wild creatures on this lake since I was born, but not always in a benign way. While I was growing up, we used to crave frog legs as much as fish dinners, but before we got to Bobs Lake in August, a man named Meyers would often have hunted the marshes heavily for them. Meyers owned a place just north of Lewis Bay, which he called Big Augur, and that was also how people referred to the big man himself. We had to scramble for what Big Augur had left.

Early on, my dad realized that I was much better at sighting a frog than he was. Beginning when I was eight and he was in his fifties, he liked to take me with him on sultry afternoons and motor up to a marshland called Michael's Creek, where the bullfrogs would be sitting stupidly in the swamp, thinking they were invisible. They're much too heavy to sit on lily pads the way children's books portray them. They float amidst the swamp greenery, only their flat heads with their googly eyes visible above the surface.

My dad would pole us in close with an oar, while I knelt in the bow and pointed them out to him. When he'd shot them, if they were too far into the dense weeds to reach them with a net, he'd send me over the side and into the muck to retrieve them like a bird dog. I was terrified of leeches but would never admit this to my father. Sometimes he'd shoot at a frog and miss (his eyesight was poor, and he was never a good shot), but it didn't bother the frog at all. It would stay right where it was until my dad got it right, and we'd bring home a "mess" of frogs, cut off their heads and webbed hands and feet, gut them, and strip off their skins. The skin of a frog parts easily from its body, leaving something that looks uncannily human. My mother would fry them just as she did fish, but as their tendons contracted, they'd twitch in the pan as though they were still alive.

I took for granted all the killing I witnessed as a child, except for one form of slaughter that disturbed me. Snapping turtles abound in our lake, chunky and huge, with a shell typically growing to fourteen inches in diameter. They are very ugly, dark all over, mossy, with jagged tails as long as their shells. This tail can be used to pick up the snapper if it's not full-grown and if you keep its plastron side toward your leg so that it can't bite you. In open water they're harmless, but on land they're aggressive and fast, raising themselves by their hind legs and pushing forward with jaws open to inflict a bite that can snap off a finger.

Turtles can be made into soup, and my dad was determined to catch them. On a summer vacation here with Dorothea before I was born, he set traps in what Laura Lee called "the Drowned Lands," one of the swamps created when the lake was dammed, flooding the woods. He caught one of the monsters, but by then it was time for my parents to begin their long, hot journey back to Ohio. He decided to transport it alive, putting it in a box on the floor inside the cabin for their last night here. During the night the turtle got out of the box and clunked around on the wooden floor, so my dad had to get up, light a kerosene lamp, find the turtle, and put it back into the box, weighing the lid down more heavily. Again it happened, but in the morning, undeterred, he put the box on the ledge behind the driver's side of the Plymouth two-passenger coupe. As usual, Dorothea was driving. During the trip—luckily—my father looked back just in time to see the turtle's jaws a few inches from my mother's neck. She always seemed amused when she told me this story. I wasn't the only one he inspired to be brave.

I was young when my dad was frogging with Hughie and another man in a swamp and glimpsed a large turtle swimming next to the boat. Spontaneously, he grabbed a rear leg and hauled the beast into the boat, probably forty pounds worth of trouble. Hughie, barefoot so that he could step out into the water for frogs, leaped onto the bow of the boat, hollering, "Where's me boots?! Where's me boots?!" about which my dad laughed for years. They came down the lake to the island shouting and waving their hats.

The turtle's protection is to withdraw its head and legs into its shell, so the men put it on the dock and jabbed its withdrawn head with a stick to get it to bite. While the turtle's neck was thus extended, my dad would come down on it with a hatchet. The first time he hit it, the blade bounced off the thick skin. The turtle was poked mercilessly until it bit again, and he struck it again. At the third stroke, blood filled its eyes and came out its nose and mouth. That, and the way they tricked it into participating in its demise, horrified me. I turned and ran into the cabin and would not come out until they'd butchered it. My mother had filmed the killing with her movie camera. I never watched my dad kill a turtle again, and whenever that film was shown, I would leave the room. No soup for me, although my mother once persuaded me to taste some fried turtle meat, and I had to admit it was good.

In my dad's world, human indifference to the suffering of animals was common. When Hughie was the fishing guide for my parents, he gutted and skinned the fish alive, fingers in the gills for a good grip, and my father followed suit. My mother showed me how to do it more mercifully, cutting through the spinal cord and beheading them before tearing them apart. It's hard to locate the spine behind the gills in the thickest part of the fish and our knives were always dull, but I did it her way when I fished.

After my dad died, I discovered his cruelty to muskrats when I found a jar of the poison he kept in the boathouse.

* * *

I've often thought it was a good thing my dad didn't have a son. I'm not sure there would have been room for two male egos in my family. However, it may not be fair of me to speculate about how my dad would have raised a boy. All I can say is that, in some ways, I believe my dad treated me as the son he would have preferred. He wouldn't let me be a coward. I was just a few years old when, here in the cabin, I poured my breakfast cereal into a bowl and found it crawling with big black ants, rendering it inedible in my opinion. Daddy plucked them out with his hand and told me to eat it. I did as I was told.

He'd survived by being a rebel but he wasn't going to allow any rebelliousness in me. For the most part he let my mother raise me, but if I disobeyed my mother, he stepped in. One morning, when I was in the early days of elementary school, I told my mother that I wasn't going to school that day. She pushed me out the door, but I hid behind a tree. When she came out to talk to me, I spoke defiantly to her.

Then my dad got involved and told me to get going and see him after school. I went. I hoped he'd forgotten about what he'd said, but when I got home, he was waiting for me and told me to go upstairs to my room and lie face down on the bed. He came with a board, told me to lower my pants and spanked me with the board. When he was finished, he made me kiss him. Later, my mother, seeing splinters on the bed, asked me what he had done, but she didn't tell me he was wrong. That sealed his authority. I didn't disobey my mother again.

It seems to me that children are born to be conflicted. A father and mother will teach and love us in different ways. A child can be seen as the prize in a popularity contest. Which parent will the child choose to favor? Why did I admire my father to the point of wanting to be like him? I loved my mother, but love and fear are closely related. I accepted my father's authority and both feared and adored him. But what if I had been a son?

Before he met my mother, my dad had been a Boy Scout leader, taking boys camping and teaching them skills. I must have been a disappointment to him. I was the youngest and smallest child in my class in elementary school in Kent, and when I said there was a girl who was bullying me, my dad tried to teach me to box, demonstrating that if I stepped on the girl's foot, she would put her weight back onto her other foot, exposing her midriff. I was to punch her in the solar plexus, knocking the wind out of her but not otherwise hurting her. Thank goodness I never tried this, but it did help. I approached her with more confidence from then on, and she stopped targeting me. For years I watched the Friday night fights with my dad on *The Cavalcade of Sports*, with its famous Gillette Blue Blades jingle.

As I grew older, I discovered that my old father, born in 1893, had old-fashioned ideas about how to raise a girl. It wasn't that he didn't care for me. He cared too much. He guarded my chastity carefully. The day a boy walked me home from high school with his arm around my shoulders, someone sighted it and reported it to my dad. It was innocent, but I wasn't allowed to see that boy again. I had no idea what my dad was afraid of. When tampons were invented, I gratefully used them, flushing them down the toilet. Then he saw one that hadn't flushed and asked my mother what it was. Oh my God! I had broken my hymen with tampons! I would not appear to be a virgin when I married. My husband might have me inspected before marriage. Huh?! It was straight out of a Victorian novel.

He declared that I should be educated so that I could fall back on something in case my husband-to-be died. The only professions he could think of for women were nurse, teacher, secretary, or librarian. He always spoke highly of the nuns who'd taught him but said I was too impatient to be a teacher. He insisted that I take a typing class one summer and thought I should concentrate on library science in college. Had he not died, I wonder if my father would have prevented my marriage at nineteen. Or whether I myself might have chosen not to marry before I finished college. As it was, maybe I was in a hurry to replace him with another man in my life, as in: *The King is dead, long live the King.*

9

When I next visit my mother, she tells me she's just spoken to *her* mother. I ask what her mother said, but Dorothea goes somewhere else in her confusion and doesn't answer. Dementia plays cruel tricks. Even when she'd first come east to live with me, she couldn't remember my childhood. Sometimes I'd try telling her the story of her life, but she'd look bewildered and say: "If you say so."

In the Seniors Home, the only memories that bubbled up were her very earliest ones. There were days when she'd ask about her parents, expecting them to arrive to take her home or to begin a journey. On those days she would seem to repeat things she'd been told as a child when her parents left her in the missionary children's home. Here in Sharbot Lake, she would try not to cry while saying that she must not dwell on her unhappiness. That she must try to make friends and to remember that her mother loved her and felt the separation too.

Dorothea did find some joy and comfort here with a lovely woman named Sadie. Sadie had some trouble speaking after a stroke, but, sitting next to one another on the couch all day, they communicated in a way that quite transcends language, with smiles, the holding and patting of hands, constant small attentions and murmurings that might or might not have made sense to others but consoled them. This was also a consolation to me, for I felt that what Sadie offered my mother was greater than anything I could any longer provide. Once I found them both lying on top of my mother's bed, giggling like schoolgirls. But then Sadie died, and another woman, much less charming, took her place on the couch next to Dorothea.

Now, my mother is neither of those two women I'd found

her to be after she'd remarried, her identity gradually erased by her dementia. By the time she arrived here in this Seniors Home, if I asked her, "Who is Philip Eichenlaub?" the man she'd loved so much, she'd say, "Sounds familiar but I just can't recall." Her Orange County love affair with Ronald Reagan was erased in her mind as well.

I like to think of my mother as I knew her with my dad here on the island: a strong, beautiful, kind woman who was always there for me. I need to compartmentalize myself, one part of me remembering her on my lovely island, and the other *me* playing the role of daughter to a dying ninety-six-year-old hunched over in a wheelchair who doesn't know who I am, or even who she herself is. I'm going to try to keep the two worlds apart, Sharbot Lake and Bobs Lake. I'll divide myself in two.

Before I return to the island, I fill a large container with drinkable water and do a little shopping. Outside the hardware store where I buy six bags of cement mix, I phone my husband's office. He's an administrator now, and often when I try to call him, I'm told he's in a meeting and can't come to the phone. Today is no exception.

I bring home a small barbecued chicken from the grocery store, and the dogs can smell it before I'm out of the boat. After we devour a whole fowl and some coleslaw for me, Ring and I settle on the couch, my lap full of dog, book propped on top of him, Blue on a rug nearby, and I enter once again into the story of the intrepid Pinkertons in *Wilderness Wife*.

The Pinkertons stayed in the far north almost five years, having a baby the third year (Kathrene went back to the States for that occasion) and using what little money they had to buy flour and a few other necessities. The log home they built for themselves was snug enough for them to withstand cold as low as fifty-six degrees below zero Fahrenheit. Each fall they shot, hauled, butchered, and froze moose and deer, and picked berries for sauces or jams. They cut wood and laid in supplies from the little store at the railroad stop, miles away, to last through the shut-in period when lake ice was forming. In winter they had to go everywhere on snowshoes. In spring they fished, shot grouse, planted a few vegetables in the thin soil, raised chickens and built additions to their cabin, until they had a total of six rooms and a fireplace and chimney.

The only thing the Pinkertons neglected was the writing. When they needed money for supplies, Robert scrambled to catch up, but his stories came back to him rejected. Desperate, Kathrene decided to run a trapping line to catch mink and ermine to sell to the trader at the store. She learned the skills she needed from an Ojibwa man with three wives, one at each corner of his long, triangular trapping line. First, she caught rabbits in snares and kept them frozen on the roof of the cabin in order to use parts of them as bait in the traps for the more lucrative furs.

Eventually Robert Pinkerton gave up on fiction and found success writing "outdoor" articles based upon their own experiences. Kathrene too wrote, on women's outdoor clothing, camp cooking, and "outdoor etiquette for the guidance of wives whose husbands take them camping." I can imagine hearing my mother laugh as she read that.

The Pinkertons still had trouble making ends meet. They were victims of their own success. They'd been greedy. The space they added to their house each year required more wood to keep it warm. They were burning between forty and fifty-five cords of wood a year, felling trees, hauling them from the forest, cutting, splitting, and carrying it all. Discovering that dogs can be used to haul wood and supplies, they gradually acquired a team and, during their second winter, for fifty cents a day, they took on the boarding of seventeen sled dogs for surveyors who would return for them the following summer.

With the dogs came more responsibility, more food to provide, more to worry about since sled dogs fight and kill one another. Finally, the Pinkertons had endured enough. At the end of their fifth summer, they turned their backs on "The North Woods" and instead spent the next seven years along the coast of British Columbia, living on a thirty-six-foot boat. Kathrene did not interpret this as failure. Nature, it seemed, had failed to intimidate the

Pinkertons. They were simply tired of it. They'd lived a penurious life of danger and hardship, full of cruelty and gore; but, writing to make money, Kathrene somehow described it matter-of-factly, her insouciant tone lending their lives an unlikely glamour.

I wonder why my mother has written my dad's name inside the cover of this book. Probably she gave it to him as a gift, a gift about a woman who would follow her husband anywhere and endure hardships just to be with her man. It doesn't inspire me to regard Kathrene as a strong woman—in spite of her determination and endurance. I would admire her more if either it had been *her* idea to go north, for whatever reason, or if she'd remained in Wisconsin working for the Tuberculosis Society and sent her husband some money to enjoy his hermitage.

One wonders what reason Kathrene's husband had for choosing to run from civilization at all, unless it was to reassure himself that he wasn't ill, or to see if his wife would follow him anywhere. I'm sure she said, *"Oh, sure! When do we start? I'd just love to scratch out a primitive living on the cold land near the arctic circle."* She was the ultimate man-pleaser. But, while he was supposedly the writer, she turned the experience into a book.

Of course, both Kathrene and Laura Lee Davidson had courage, and I admire that in them both, but I feel less empathy with Kathrene than with Laura Lee. Kathrene was tough and had more reason to kill animals than my dad ever did, but her writing conveys no compensating pleasures in return for living hard like that. Understandably, she's concentrating upon survival, not the beauty of her surroundings, but one wonders why she and Robert had chosen to live that way. Her talk of wild creatures is all aimed toward acquisition of their meat or fur. She makes no note of birds except when she found an owl in a trap and says, oblivious to her own predatory behavior, "Shooting an owl was a pleasure. Those assassins of the woods dive murderously on a victim each day in the year." When Robert shot a deer, they celebrated by eating its liver that night. They were becoming feral, whereas Laura Lee had a romantic sensibility, lovingly observing eighty-five years ago the ancestors of the wild creatures I see now. She felt the same thrill I

do at the rising of the full moon at setting sun. I can understand
why she came here alone and kept coming back.

10

I'm not a woman of the wilderness. I can romanticize my weeks in the wild because I can escape when the going gets rough. I have a choice. But some women have hardship imposed upon them, with no hope of escape, and rise to great heights of resilience and endurance, like Harriet Lewis. I once took a notebook over to the farmhouse and wrote down what Hughie Lewis told me about his mother.

Harriet Campsall and Hughie's father, Hugh Lewis, married and bought this farm of 185 acres in 1867, for $250. When the lake was first dammed, it marooned the Lewises on their farm, cutting them off from the road just four years after they'd bought the land and cleared the fields. They were never compensated for the loss.

Harriet had seven children and lost her husband to pneumonia when the oldest was just thirteen. Hughie, the youngest, had not yet been born and never saw his father. Harriet remained on the farm, raising her children by keeping a garden, cows, chickens, turkeys, geese, pigs, sheep, oxen at first, and later, horses. In the spring they sheared the sheep for wool. She used some of the wool to make socks and sweaters, and traded wool for cloth. She raised wheat and had it ground into flour in Westport. She raised corn for cornmeal. To reach a road, they rowed across the entrance of Mud Bay to Mica Point where they kept a buggy, making a horse swim on a rope behind the boat. On the other side they hitched the horse to the buggy, drove all those miles to the store in Westport and back, and unhitched the horse. It would always swim home by itself, Hughie said, not even stopping to eat a mouthful of grass.

Harriet baked her own bread. Her cows were dairy cows and

she sold butter for groceries. She harvested maple syrup and used some for syrup, some for sugar. The basswood trees on the farm made troughs for the syrup and branches of sumac the hollow tubes for the sap spoil. The boys hunted and fished and salted pork and herring. The family made pot ash for soap, burning hard wood to boil ash to make lye. The huge iron kettle in which the ash was boiled is still here on the farm.

In 1892 the oldest boy discovered mica on their land. Anything below ground "belonged to the Crown," so the family was never paid for the use of their land, which was mined well into the twentieth century. No road was built to the mine, all equipment being brought in and all produce taken out by boat. The Lewises did benefit from a telephone line that serviced the mine, and the mine employed local people, including Harriet, who cooked for the men.

Hughie was the only one of Harriet's children who didn't move away. In those days young people met at country dances. Hughie heard tunes played around the lake, bought himself a fiddle and taught himself to play by ear. He learned square dances, round dances, and step dance. During the First World War, when he was twenty-eight, Hughie went west on the Canadian Pacific Railway to work on the harvest in Saskatchewan, perhaps as a stab at leaving home, but he returned to this farm the same year.

When Wilson bought the peninsula from the Lewises in 1920 and hired him as overseer, the work brought Hughie enough money to build a new house. The log cabin Hughie's father had built had no view of the lake, being over the hill, halfway between Lewis Bay and Mud Bay near a grove of apple trees. Harriet said she would never move out of it.

Building a house without road access isn't easy. Hughie chose a site on the crest of the hill looking east over Lewis Bay and hired a carpenter, a Swede named Cornelius Granlin. It took two days to dig out the cellar by hand. Its cement walls are one foot thick. There is a well in the cellar that taps a spring and has never run dry. The old house had no well; they'd carried water up from the pump at the mines. Harriet sat on a rock near the old house and said she'd never go over to the new one.

It was tight and compact. They put in a floor of birch, with the main room overlooking the lake, three small bedrooms along the back, and an attic room over all. At the north end of the house a summer kitchen was added, and at the south end, a set of cement steps led to the front door. When the house began to take shape, old Mrs. Lewis appeared with a chair to sit in while she talked to the men. She came every day after that, and each time she left, there would be another piece of furnishing at the new house. The old cabin became a barn.

Soon after that, Hughie married a pretty girl, Sarah Elizabeth MacVeigh of Sharbot Lake, always called "Lizzie," whom he'd hired to help his aged mother with the work. Harriet occupied the middle bedroom and soon there were two boys in the third, Keith and Ervin. Harriet lived to be ninety-six, and two years before she died, there was a third and final child, Joan, my summer playmate.

My dad knew Harriet when she was in her nineties and admired her. She told him she'd once seen seven bears swim together from her land to our island and on to Bear Island, which is probably when it got its name. Dorothea caught her in a photo, the apotheosis of a wilderness wife, her head covered with a small black shawl pinned beneath her chin.

In contrast, I'm reminded of Susanna Moodie, an English woman who followed her husband to a homestead in Ontario in the 1830s. At the end of her account of their grueling experience, *Roughing It in the Bush*, she wrote:

If these sketches should prove the means of deterring one family from sinking their property, and shipwrecking all their hopes, by going to reside in the backwoods of Canada, I shall consider myself amply repaid for revealing the secrets of the prison-house, and feel that I have not toiled and suffered in the wilderness in vain.

Hugh, Keith, Lizzie, Ervin and Harriet Lewis

* * *

Laura Lee Davidson never again wintered on Bobs Lake, but her American friends feared she might "go native" canoeing around in the northern woods each summer. They need not have worried. She would never be tolerant of what she called "the bucolic mind," which she thought "almost totally devoid of imagination." While she prided herself on her ability to understand the local dialect and the ways of the "natives," Laura Lee wrote of them in *Winter of Content*: "Strange people, at once so old and so young, so instructed in vice and sorrow, and so ignorant of the simplest teachings of life."

She once remarked to her friend who owned Mica Island: "Living in the midst of beauty like this should do something for the soul, and yet I don't believe the people here see it. How do you account for the sordid outlook of the dwellers in places like this?"

Her friend replied:

I suppose that if every sunset reminded you that the pig must be fed and the cows milked, if every time you looked out of a window you saw the hawks after the young chickens, or the horse trampling the corn, and if you always had to go to bed at dusk in order to get up the next morning at four o'clock to plow, the beauty of it all would not be the first thought in your mind.

Laura Lee sort of concedes: "Perhaps not."

And yet, what I value most in her writing are her descriptions of Harriet. She tells us: "She was a beauty once. She is a pretty old woman still, with her flashing black eyes and silver hair." And she marvels at how, in addition to everything else, Harriet found time to make wonderful patchwork quilts.

The name Laura Lee had chosen for the Lewises in her books was a French-sounding one, "Drapeau." They resented being given a French name, especially one that meant "curtains," but she seems to have admired Harriet, judging by this report of a visit to the Lewis farm:

In spite of hard work and advancing years, Mrs. Drapeau is active still. I rowed over yesterday to buy some eggs and, hearing a great commotion in the pasture, wandered on to see what was going forward. She was helping the men to round up a cow and her calf, preparatory to selling them to Alf Henderson, who was waiting to swim them over to mainland. Everyone was running round and round the field, men were shouting, cow lowing, calf bellowing, the bull roaring and threatening to break down the paling round his enclosure. When Mrs. Drapeau caught sight of me she laid her hands on the top rail of the fence, and with the ease of a lad, she vaulted over....

When the cow was finally caught we followed her and her captors down the hill to the shore to watch them away. The men climbed into a leaky old punt, laid the calf in at their feet, and pushed off. After a moment's frantic bellowing the cow, poor creature, waded out after them and away across the narrow bay they all went, old Bess swimming desperately, and soon all we could see of her were the tips of her horns and the whites of her terrified eyes. As we climbed the steep hill to the house I looked at Mrs. Drapeau: she was not even breathing fast.

* * *

Outside, the sun is swelling to the west, sending its softened light glancing off the water and up onto the undersides of leaves, turning the islands into shimmering green and gold. Everything that flies through the air, from midges to osprey, is touched softly with this golden light. I feel as though I'm in a Maxfield Parrish painting. It must be said that nothing Laura Lee nor I have observed and admired on this lake is missed by the "native" I know best. Ervin, sitting contentedly over there on his hill with June, seeing it all, has told me he doesn't dream of being anywhere else.

11

Each year the doctor who owns the Seniors Home entertains the residents and their relatives on the grounds of his beautiful estate overlooking a bay on the north shore of Sharbot Lake. The director of the Seniors Home organizes games on the lawn with prizes, drawing everyone in and lifting the elderly up out of themselves. People who can't walk can toss water-filled balloons, getting wet but having a good time. There's a prize for guessing the number of jellybeans in a jar. Musical chairs is played by passing something around, stopping the music, and wheeling away the player holding the object, until only one person is left. There's plenty of good picnic food and musical entertainment. The doctor takes professional-quality photos of all the residents to update the portraits in the Home, and a few staff members get thrown into the lake by other staff members.

For most of the residents it's a great treat to get out of the Home, to let the walls come down and be out of doors, but one year my mother found it so disorienting that she spent most of the time crying, worrying that she would be left in the woods. She didn't know who I was, and when I assured her that I was there to take care of her, she thanked me profusely for "helping" her.

The following year, she and I remained in the Home on picnic day, and another woman, Margery, stayed in as well, a victim of Alzheimer's. There we three were in the parlor, everything gone quiet. To break the silence, I opened my mother's 1932 Methodist Hymnal. I grew up in the Methodist church, where my mother was a soloist and conductor of the youth choir. I looked for a hymn I could pick up the tune for, sightreading a first line. Already Margery had it and could sing the words, leading the way through the first verse, sometimes the second.

As we sang one hymn after another, my mother listened to my prompts and the old familiar phrases came to her, too, though not as freely as they did to Margery. She, like my mother, didn't know where she was or when, talked of strange events in words that didn't follow one another in logical sequence, yet the words to hymns came to her connected not just to the tune but, when the tune repeated, in the correct sequence of verses.

I searched for what I knew were my mother's favorites. Each time we came to the end of one of these, Dorothea would say, "Beautiful. Just beautiful." The old gospel hymns of the nineteenth century were comforting to her because they were familiar in spite of her loss of memory, but also because they are songs of love. We sang, "What a friend we have in Jesus." Margery began, "Softly and tenderly Jesus is calling . . . ." We sang: "I've found a Friend, O such a Friend! He loved me ere I knew Him." And an old favorite of Mother's:

I walk in the garden alone while the dew is still on the roses
And the voice I hear calling on my ear the Son of God discloses.
Oh, He walks with me, and He talks with me,
And He tells me I am His own
And the joy we share as we tarry there
None other shall ever know.

For a young woman born around 1900, Jesus must have seemed the perfect love, the ideal helpmate. How many women, after the promises of such pure love, were disappointed by real life unions?

Jesus, Thy boundless love to me
No thought can reach, no tongue declare;
O knit my thankful heart to Thee,
And reign without a rival there!
Thine wholly, Thine alone, I'd live,
Myself to Thee entirely give.

This sweet singing was the closest thing to joy my mother, or Margery, had left, and I found pleasure in bringing it to them. When the others returned from the picnic, they were treated to smiles from Dorothea, glimpses of the personality she once had.

Margery is gone now, defeated by her disease. This year, when I arrive in Sharbot Lake on picnic day to keep Dorothea company, the Home is abuzz, picnic-goers gathered in the foyer, a traffic jam of aluminum walkers, everyone with a sun hat. Two members of the staff stand by the door of the bus to hoist people up the steps. Others load walkers and wheelchairs into a truck. The most handicapped are loaded into a special van.

Dorothea is in the parlor, in a Geri Chair today, tilted about half-way back, her eyes closed. On the attached tray there's a can of Ensure with a straw stuck through the top. We have the house nearly to ourselves. Ruby is the staff member left in charge of us and two or three other residents, who prefer to remain in their rooms.

I smooth lotion into my mom's dry skin and encourage her to take little sips of Ensure. I try humming some tunes as I think of them, or talking about old times, but she responds to nothing except to wince when I try to brush her still-thick head of pure white hair. She wants to sleep in her comfortable chair. I talk with kind, gentle Ruby, who stops to check on us once in a while, but mainly I sit and feel useless. It's no picnic. There, with my mother, a strange sensation comes to me, something I never feel when I'm alone. I feel lonely.

12

The weather has turned hot, not so bad on the lake, but in the evenings heat lightning pulses to the east beyond the islands, very bright, like explosions with no sound. In the middle of the heat wave, the radio invites listeners to send in suggestions of winter songs celebrating cold, so we hear "Sleigh bells ring, are you listening?" and "Jack Frost's nipping at your nose." Then, as a gray cloud passes, a smattering of rain changes the smell and feel of the air. Blue lifts her head and drinks it in, but the relief is short-lived and the day hotter than ever. On the radio later a mention of tornado warnings for eastern Ontario, so I spend some time thinking about where I would ride out a tornado here in this old cabin, picturing the logs lifting off one by one.

Ms. Hummingbird has put the finishing touches on her nest, sticking pale green lichen on its sides, making it look so much like cedar bark that, if it weren't for the hum of her coming and going, I'd never find it. Probably the lichen waterproofs it too. Though the hummingbird is the smallest bird of all, her nest seems small even for her, perhaps an inch and a half across at its widest. I find in a book that she has a wingbeat rate of twenty-five per second. When she lays her two white eggs, her heartbeat will slow and her body temperature drop so that she can brood.

Ervin has a day off from working at Nordlaw, and he's come to have his yearly visit with me. With Ring between us, we sit on the porch and drink Coca-Cola. Time was when a young Ervin carried a case of beer in his boat to drink all day, but years ago he decided to quit and hasn't had another drink since, though he kept beer in the house for his dad as long as Hughie was alive. Ervin gave up smoking the same way.

When his parents were aging and his young daughter was reaching school age, Ervin bought a house on the road at Bolingbroke where the family lives in cold months, returning here to the lake in the summers. In order to tend his stock in winter, he must cross the pass from Mica Point daily, often walking across ice. He has to be many things as a farmer—vet, mechanic, carpenter, roofer, plumber, lumberjack, gardener, hunter, butcher—and he's in high demand as a fishing guide on the lake, just as his father was.

Ervin has spent the morning working to repair the fence where his small herd of cows broke through onto property to the south. He doesn't complain about this chore but rather observes equitably that cows are "very inquisitive." Since I've decided that I'm on a quest to understand my having always wanted to be like my father, I ask him about the old days. Ervin and his older brother Keith knew a somewhat different side of my dad than I did. Keith, who married an American and moved to Ohio years ago, said to me on one of his infrequent visits home, "You're like him and that's not all bad." My dad had found Keith a much better pupil for boxing than I was, later regretting teaching him when he heard that Keith had thrown a punch at Hughie. Of the two boys, both of my parents favored Ervin

The Lewises—Hughie, Lizzie, Keith and Ervin

When Ervin was perhaps ten, my dad thought it was time for him to learn to shoot, so he brought out his gun. Looking around for a target, he sighted a pair of loons. Before the lesson was over, they'd shot one and brought it from the lake onto the dock, placing it as though it was swimming there. My mother took a picture.

Ervin is holding the loon's head up and I, five years old in a white dress and a white ribbon in my hair, am holding out one of its wings. I ask him if he remembers that picture. My mother took a lot of photos in those days and sent copies to the Lewises.

Oh yes, he remembers that day.

Unlike my dad's, Ervin's life has been one of hunting, fishing, and trapping as a livelihood. Existence here demanded it. He's not sentimental, but I know that both of us love having the loons in our bay. His attitude about my dad always seems to be ambivalent. So I ask him now, "Why do you think he chose a loon to shoot at?" No one ever eats loons.

He stares out at the channel in front of us where the loon had been. "It ate his fish? He needed a target?"

Ervin tells me that the following autumn when Phil came back to the lake, he called Hughie as usual from a general store a few miles from the garage on the mainland. In those days, before my dad built our garage, we stored our boat on the island. Hughie would launch our boat and row it across the lake, where my dad would attach his seven horsepower Martin. But this time Phil told Hughie to bring Ervin along because he had something for him. The "something" was a 12-gauge Winchester pump shotgun, an army weapon, brand new, never used.

"It was two inches taller than I was," Ervin says.

Ervin became part of the hunting parties. In those days deer were scarce and they usually hunted ducks in the fall, but one year, according to Ervin, after a round of Seagram's King's Plate for the men, Phil and Ervin went to hunt black squirrels on Lewis land, while Hughie took the others south to Timmerman's Island. Ervin took his dog, who could find and tree any squirrel on the farm. A lone hunter has trouble shooting a squirrel because the squirrel will always move around the trunk to the opposite side, out of sight. Phil would go around behind the tree to drive the squirrel into Ervin's sights where he could shoot it. Ervin laughs. "The others got nothing. When they came back, they found nine squirrels laid out on the porch. Each one shot through the head."

They all ate squirrel for supper. Ervin says you cook them by boiling them with soda until they're nearly tender, then frying them. My dad brought me two of the black squirrel tails to hang from the handlebars of my bicycle, something my friends in Kent thought was . . . well, *strange*.

Ervin remembers that there was one man who relieved my dad at the stove in the early days, Ray Salvatore, who ran the bar in Kent called Ray's. One time when Ray cooked spaghetti, he sent a pail of it home with Hughie for the kids, something they'd never tasted before. "Oh, it was good," Ervin says, remembering, then repeats it: "It was good."

I ask if he remembers teaching Joan and me to frog here in the swampy cove of Lewis Bay when we were children. It's not necessary to *shoot* them. Ervin showed us how to catch what we called "field frogs" for bait, actually little leopard frogs, bright green speckled with black, that leapt around in the grasses on the hillside. He put them into a minnow bucket with the lid on, and we poled his boat into the thick weeds with an oar.

Using a stick, we tied fishline around the waist of a leopard and dangled it in front of a bullfrog, who'd remain motionless for a while as though the small one wasn't there, then all of a sudden shoot forward to take it in his mouth. After waiting until he'd settled again and begun to swallow the leopard, we hauled him into the boat. The frog wouldn't let go of his easy prize. If he did drop off the bait into the water, we just offered it to him again, and again he'd take it.

Ervin would hold the bullfrog by the hind legs and swing its head against the edge of the boat to kill it, then toss it into a second minnow bucket. We repeated the process, reusing the same leopard unless it was too mangled to tie securely, until we had enough to eat or until we could no longer find big enough frogs. Ervin gave them all to me to take home. I don't think the Lewis family ate frogs.

"My dad was impressed when I brought frogs home without a gun," I tell Ervin.

He laughs and says, "He'd shoot anything."

"I seldom hear a frog anymore."

"No. Their numbers are down."

Later, cleaning out a drawer in Marian Wilson's old buffet, I discover my dad's State of Ohio resident Hunter's and Trapper's licenses, from 1926 through 1948. During those twenty-two years, the cost for a license to kill remained constant at one dollar. In 1926 and 1927, for ten days in November, you were allowed to shoot three pheasants a day ("cock birds only"). By 1928 the limit was two pheasants. In those first two years you could bag ruffed grouse, up to three in one day, but after that they were "protected, no open season."

You could shoot twenty-five ducks, geese, coot, or gallinule in any one day. The beautiful wood duck, however, was protected, as were deer, whose numbers were very low then. The licenses directed:

Landowners and farmers are requested to grant permission to hunt to those who ask permission if possible. A day afield is a real treat to those who are penned up in office or factory most of the time. The hunters and fishermen, thru (sic) their license money, are paying for all the work of restocking with fish or game and for all the activities of the Fish and Game Division, without the cost of a cent to the taxpayers.

But you couldn't hunt on Sundays.

There was no limit on the number of foxes you could kill in

1926 and '27, from November through January. It was the same for raccoons, although they were protected in the daytime. This lasted until 1928, when raccoons were lumped together with opossum, foxes, and skunks, with no limit. They are all considered just "varmint." Most passerines (songbirds) were protected, but:

Crows, Great-horned Owls, English Sparrows, Chicken Hawks, American Goshawks, Blue Hawks, Cooper Hawks, Sharp Shinned Hawks, and Duck Hawks may be killed any time except Sunday. Black birds may be killed at any time except Sunday when doing damage.

In the 1930s, the game laws remain more or less the same, although the numbers of ducks, geese, and gallinule which may be taken are reduced and a federal permit is required for "baiting" wild ducks and geese. In 1938 the red fox is protected outside of a season from November 15 to February 1, but a "gray fox may be taken or had in possession at any time," and there is a bounty on crows: "Take crow heads to township clerk."

In the early twentieth century the common loon was protected in Canada, but according to Laura Lee Davidson, even then one would now and then see a boat cushion made of the skin and beautiful feathers of the loon. Now, affected by swallowing lead weights used for fishing tackle in the northern lakes, and floating oil and mercury in the South where they winter, their numbers have declined, with very few still breeding in the United States. An article in the Kingston, Ontario, paper not long ago says four loons had been sighted around that area with fish line dangling from their bills, having eaten a fish with a hook in it.

13

When my daughter Molly was a teenager, she and I came here to the cabin one spring to paint the floors. On an overcast afternoon, we heard strange cries and something beating the surface of the lake between Bear Island and Goose Island. We motored around the little island and found two loons in a life-or-death struggle, one holding the other down in the water by the neck. I aimed the boat right at them to break up the fight.

Both loons moved toward Bear Island, one making anguished sounds and heading for shore, the other giving chase. I cut the motor and we followed into shallow water, Molly at the oars, trying to come between them. Our presence forced the pursuer to rise and beat his wings forward at us, thumping his chest. After uttering his tremulous cry, he dove and swam beneath us, at least three feet from the tip of his bill to the end of his paddling feet, heading for open water.

The other loon had worked its way along shore to a place where it could crawl up and lie under a tree. We rowed close to see what injuries it might have, but it was lying prone with no obvious marks, head flat to the ground, breathing heavily like a dog panting. The one behind us hooted and Molly shouted at him, "Go away, big bully!"

The loon near us on the ground uttered a mournful quaver. "Quiet!" we said. Molly leaned forward for a closer look at the red eye in its sleek black head, a crisp collar of white with vertical black stripes around its neck above a band of dark iridescent green, but the loon drew its feet beneath it to rise. We backed off, sitting in the boat off shore, protecting it.

For a while it was a standoff, the other loon patrolling farther out. "Go fish, you bird brain!" I yelled at him. This struck Molly as funny.

"See, you can't get away with it, you feather-brained maniac," she added, and we hung around being silly, laughing so hard the boat created halos on the surface of the lake. The loon under the tree remained quite still.

The clouds darkened and it began to rain, and the big bad loon gliding around the bay with his mate seemed to have lost his murderous intentions. Still, we sat on in the drizzle, drifting within view of our island, which floated in the mist above the rain-flattened water like a cool San Giorgio Maggiore. I asked Molly if she remembered seeing that old picture of me with Ervin and the loon my dad had shot.

"I always thought that was disgusting," she said.

"Well, things were different then," I offered.

"Why did he shoot it?" she asked.

I couldn't really say.

"You always admired your father," she said, half accusingly.

"Yes," I said. "I did."

How does one explain? An issue like this can *seem* black or white.

When we returned a few hours later to check on it, the loon under the tree was gone. My dad taught me about the thrill of the kill, but the thrill of the save is equal to it.

What should I think now about a father who killed and made me a killer too? It's clear to me now that, like my mother, my dad was also two different people for me. A professional in a white shirt most of the year, and an exuberant outdoorsman every August, when life suddenly burst into technicolor with a frantic search for something to kill. Had he not bought the island in Canada, I might have two-dimensional, sepia-toned memories of my dad instead of the vivid images I have today. For three weeks each year, for me, Daddy was action. Daddy was exciting. I was his apprentice. Mommy came out of the kitchen now and then to see what we were up to before returning to her drudgery.

It's almost a cliché, isn't it: fathers and daughters? It was not my ambition to be like my mom. She didn't have the leisure to sunbathe on the dock as I do now. My only memories of her on the dock were on the days when she did laundry, using a large washtub into which she poured lake water that she'd heated on the stove. She had a long-handled metal plunger for agitating the clothes in the tub with some laundry soap powder. There was a scrubbing board and a large cake of brown soap for attacking dirt. Finally, she'd dunk each article in the lake and swish it around to rinse before wringing it out by hand. After dumping the wash water into the lake, she'd carry the tub full of the wet clothes to the clothesline. People were not generally aware in those days of the ill effect of pollution on a working lake. My parents were of their time.

As for my dad and the killing, it was a manly thing to provide food for the table, and most of what my dad killed we ate, but killing was considered "sport" in those days. My dad subscribed to magazines like *Outdoor Life* and *Field and Stream*, both of which glorified hunting and fishing. Guns were like wallpaper while I was growing up. Next to my bedroom in Kent was the gun room. Old guns decorated the cabin. The walls and shutters of the cabin displayed pictures celebrating the hunt.

My dad led me to take all this for granted, but I'm a person of *my* time, aware of the need to preserve a balance in nature and learning to respect other forms of life. It's the memory of things like poisoning the muskrats or shooting at woodpeckers or a loon that finally broke into the smug complacency of my hero worship.

An experience I had when I was sixteen failed to produce an epiphany at the time. During the Great Depression and before he married Dorothea, Phil was robbed. By then he'd bought the house in Kent where I grew up, large enough for both his office rooms and living quarters. Two men were in the waiting room and, when he came out to greet them, they told him to go upstairs to his bedroom where they took his wallet and warned him not to follow them. He always had money on him, for patients paid him in cash. Only when they'd gone did it occur to him that his WWI service pistol, a Colt M1911 semi-automatic .45, was in the bedroom, and he had not thought of it during the robbery.

Probably because of that experience, the .45 became a fixture hanging from the bedpost on my dad's side of their bed. One fall, while I was a teenager, my mom and dad decided to go together to Canada in October, trusting me enough to leave me at home attending school, with a girlfriend named Gail staying in the house with me. Gail and I loved the independence—having the whole house to ourselves, and one night, tucked away in my parents' bed, I drew the gun out of its holster and showed it to Gail. Quite comfortable with it at first and confident that it wasn't loaded, I pulled back the hammer just as I would on a toy cowboy cap pistol. But then I couldn't release it.

I didn't want my father to know that I'd been playing around with his gun, so I had to get the thing uncocked and replace it as I'd found it. Apparently, however, the only way to release the hammer was to pull the trigger. I aimed at the floor beside the bed just in case, then paused to imagine what would happen if it were *not* unloaded. The bullet would go through the rug and floor and arrive somewhere in the dining room below. It *couldn't* be loaded, I told Gail, and almost pulled the trigger. But it seemed too big a thing and I laid the gun on the table next to the bed and went to sleep.

The next day, still fearful that my dad would be angry with me, I still couldn't get up my nerve to pull the trigger. The gun looked nothing like my old lean, curved, toy six-shooters. It was squarish, heavy, not silver but dark and menacing. I decided to get help.

We lived very close to the center of town and at the corner of our street was a Western Auto store, owned by friends of my parents. Their adult son, Bill, worked in the store, and I liked him. I drew him out to the driveway behind the store and asked him to pull the trigger for me, assuring him it was not a *loaded* gun but that I just needed to release the hammer so that my father would not find me out. I remember his hesitating, but the Western Auto sold guns, so he was used to handling them, and, after all, I'd assured him it wasn't loaded.

The blast created a crater in the asphalt at least a foot across, whipped his arm back painfully, boomed largely, echoing off city buildings . . . and the hammer was still cocked.

Leaving Bill in shock, I took this *loaded* war weapon and headed around the corner and down the busy street to the main square in town where a cop often stood next to the traffic light box. Sure enough, Mr. Thompson was standing there in uniform. I knew his girls from school. He didn't say anything when I explained what I wanted him to do: lower the hammer. He unloaded the gun somehow and handed it and its magazine back to me in two pieces. On one hand, I was relieved because the thing was disarmed, but on the other, I knew that now my dad would find out and I'd be in big trouble.

As it was, when my parents returned and I told them, before others could, my mom turned on my father and blamed *him* for leaving the gun loaded. All those years it had been there next to his head, ripe and ready to kill, and I guess she hadn't realized it. Nothing much was said to me about it after that, and I don't believe I ever told them how close I'd come to shattering the floor of their bedroom.

14

It's Dorothea's ninety-seventh birthday! All it means for her is more of the same, really, although I've brought her a new sweater, Joan has sent flowers, and the cook has baked a sheet cake. At the end of the noon meal everyone gets a square of the cake with ice cream. Dorothea's piece is brought with a candle in it, and people sing the birthday song. The older ones look confused when they get to the line where a name is required.

Dorothea hasn't wanted to eat at all. Still, she manages to blow out the candle and eat some of her cake and ice cream with a crushed vitamin pill. The only thing she says is "mm mm" when I put ice cream in her mouth. She's clearly undernourished, yet the weaker she becomes, the less she cares to try.

I show my mother photos of my daughter Molly's two children: Helen, at her birthday party, just turned two. William will soon be four. Dorothea smiles, seeing the lovely children, but she doesn't comprehend that the blonde-haired boy and the girl blowing out candles are her own great-grandchildren.

After the meal, the staff puts her into bed for a nap and I call my husband. This time he's in his office. He tells me what's going on in his life. I tell him about my mother, though he hasn't asked. Before we hang up, I ask him if he thinks he'll come here this summer. As usual: Maybe. Maybe not.

Joan arrives to pick me up. We have lunch at The Beach House on the shore of Sharbot Lake. Joan remembers that while we were growing up, my mother would give a little birthday party for her in our cabin every August 13, baking a cake and making tapioca pudding as a substitute for the ice cream we couldn't keep frozen. Her mom would come, but there were no other children to play with anywhere near the Lewis farm. These parties were very special for

Joan, and she loved my mother for it.

* * *

It has rained in the night, the wind shifted to the north, and it's chilly here on the lake. I sleep until seven when Blue gets me up with an unrefusable paw. Everything is silvery—sky, lake, even the wet green trees. Sadly, I see that something has torn the humming-bird's nest apart. Either that or she hadn't bound it well enough with webs, for fluff has escaped and hangs all around among the cedar sprays. I watch for her return to see her reaction. Squeaking like a mouse, she gathers up the fluff and replaces it, occasionally looking up, perhaps for the marauder. Such a tiny female on her own. So much responsibility!

When the coffee's made, I pour hot water into the basin of my wrought iron washstand and have a warm bath for once, then dress in jeans, a sweater, and a blue denim shirt, soft with age.

Back in the kitchen, Blue begins to drool before the bacon hits the pan. I scramble eggs and feed both dogs heartily. My collection of Fiesta Ware includes many colors, cool blue and green, light yellow, and deep purple, but I choose a loud orange plate to brighten up this dull day, and eat inside at the round table. A dog on the radio fools Ring. He has less experience than Blue with electronic sound. A stupid song about a dog named—guess what—"Blue" features a rhythmic barking and some howling. The radio is on a windowsill between the porch and the living room. Ring goes to the door and stares into the room for a while, then, when the barking is repeated, he goes outdoors and up to the cove, still looking for the mysterious dog.

I'm living essentially in the outdoors, so I close all the cabin's windows and, seeing how dirty they are, decide to wash a few of them. In mid-morning it's still cold. The best way to warm the cabin is to bake, so I mix dough and set the large oven box over two of the burners on the kerosene stove to preheat. The dogs are content to lie in the main room, watching me come and go to check the oven temperature. I lunch on warm chocolate chip cookies and make up for it by sweeping floors.

Around three, the sky looks as though someone has half-heart-edly tried to wipe it clean. The dogs, restless now with cabin fever, expect something to happen. All right, we'll have a walk in the woods above the Drowned Lands. With an old plastic bleach bottle cut to make a scoop, I bail the boat, both dogs sitting impatiently in it, and row us around into Wilson's Bay. I wonder why Blue's in the boat and not swimming. Actually, it seems that Ring is the one who wants to leap out. He's frantic, hanging out over the edge of the boat, one side then the other, perpetual motion. I pull toward the shore in order to put them out and they bound into the shallow water, both in a frenzy now. I figure they'll follow me when I push out to resume my row, Ring by land, Blue in the water, but immediately there is the most godawful screeching coming from a little stand of trees. I can't see what's happening in among the low bushes. Blue is barking and I call her insistently several times, but she doesn't stop.

I pull the boat up and am looking for a place to secure the rope when the dogs come back through the thicket, Ring proudly bringing me a young, half-grown raccoon in his mouth, shaking and biting it. I tell him to drop it and leave it, and he does, but I can see it's already mortally wounded. It can't use its hind legs, but keeps up a defense, wanting to bite me or Ring if we approach.

I know it will suffer dreadfully if left that way, so I tell Ring to finish what he's begun. "Kill it," I say to him, desperate to end its ordeal, and he shakes it. The noises are horrible, all the worse as the animal weakens. When Ring drops it, it tries to maintain a defensive watch, but it's suffering so much that it can only wait, sprawled on its back, eyes closing. I step out of the boat to find a rock with which to end this horror, but Ring brings the little raccoon into the water. Drown it! A good way to end it quickly. But after Ring has dragged it around head down in the water until I think it's gone, I think I see its mouth open when he takes it up on shore, so I order Ring to bring it back into the water. Instead, he leaps into the boat with it. At this point I grab it from him by the tail, drop it headfirst into the water, where it doesn't move, yank

Blue into the boat by her collar, and, shocked, push off.

Instead of going on, I row directly back home, both dogs riding quietly. I wonder what Blue is thinking, standing there in the boat panting, not looking at anything in particular. How does that act of killing sit with her? Her conscience is formed mainly by my rules of what she may and may not do. She did leave it all up to him. I put my hand out to her, but Ring pushes himself between us, demanding the attention for himself. His first actions upon reaching our island are to piss and hump Blue. He's very proud of himself. I'm remembering Kipling's advice:

Brothers and Sisters, I bid you beware
Of giving your heart to a dog to tear.

Disgusted with him, I pace the porch and consider taking him to the farm and putting him back on the chain. Or, better yet, strangling him with my own two hands.

After a while, I calm down and contemplate my own hypocrisy. It is, as we say, the nature of the beast. It was clear that he was doing what pleases his master. Farmers depend upon dogs and cats to protect their produce from opportunistic wildlife, and what did I originally bring Ring over here for, after all? To rid me of raccoons. He thought he was pleasing me.

The human race has a love/hate relationship with the raccoon. They're considered pests— hunted, trapped and, in suburbia, "removed," but in places where humans come into contact with the wild, it's the raccoon which first approaches and charms them. They're easily tamed, soon willing to take food from your hand. Many of the campers around here feed them, some at permanent feeders. A man down the lake named Tom would boat in fifty-pound bags of dry dog food and name and photograph his families of raccoons as though they were his grandchildren. The fat, lazy young ones that thrive on this welfare system haven't been taught how to survive a winter. The trouble is that even the most inveterate of these kind-hearted humans leave the lake in October, not to return until May. Ervin finds the young raccoons dead of starvation in his barn.

I certainly don't feed them. At first my family and I weren't aware that we shared our cabin, although we'd see them occasionally hanging on our screens, begging on their rounds. Then one year, it began to smell like an animal den under our porch, and I realized that they had set up serious housekeeping. Thus began the contest between me and the raccoons, as I would close off their entry with rocks and wire screen, only to find the following year that they'd bent the wire and displaced the rocks.

This went on for several years. Then I had a bright idea. I was here alone, no dog with me, but Ervin had a young dog, a border collie that he'd bought for his daughter, Julie. On a day when the Lewises were away, I stopped to draw drinking water for myself from their outdoor tap, giving some to the little collie, whose water bowl was empty. Afterward, I couldn't stop thinking about him over there on his chain. A few days later, having seen raccoons going under my kitchen the night before, I went back to ask Ervin if I could take Ring to the island to discourage them. He graciously said yes. "He always likes a boat ride," he told me.

That first year Ring recognized his duty right away and proceeded like gangbusters. The first thing he did when we reached the island was roll in the freshest raccoon dung. Then he went around the cabin three times, pissing everywhere he could. When it grew dark, I invited him into the cabin. He came in politely, explored it, went into my bedroom for a look, and then came out to the living room to join me. That was when he noticed a deer head coming out of the wall, the dark gloomy one over the fireplace, and he did a double take, backing up a step and growling. He growled more when he saw the others but didn't overdo it and soon joined me as if we weren't surrounded. During the night I was awakened by the sound of running, then of the porch door opening, and then short business-like barks. Ring scared off the raccoons before they could enter their den. He earns his bacon.

When Ervin came home from work the next afternoon, Ring was excited watching the boat go toward the farm, and he searched my eyes. Shouldn't he be there to greet Ervin? I reminded him that he had work to do here.

Ring slept on a mat next to my bed, went everywhere with me

during the day, and if I sat on the porch and he was outside, I had only to look up and he would be looking at me through the screen. He'd dabble along the shore while I worked on my rock wall, and was gymnastic at catching flies but didn't know them from bees. A fussy eater, he was very delicate in his manners, taking food very gently, and he'd put his paw on what I was doing to get attention. No animal will work more willingly for a human than a border collie, and none will demand more love in return.

A week later we had a hard night. At one a.m. I heard Ring go out the door. For half an hour he periodically rushed and barked. Not a lot—he's not a barker. These would be followed by a splash of something hitting the surface of the water, apparently from a height. It sounded as if we were being bombarded by cannonballs. I let him handle it. I figured anything so persistent must be either human or raccoon. If it were human, I didn't want to know. I had no gun with which to threaten anyone. My dad's .22 was hanging on a rack in Ervin's kitchen. I lay on my back so I could hear but tried to go to sleep. Just as I'd relax and think it was over . . . more cannonballs. The scenario I devised in my half-asleep state was that all twenty-five of Tom's raccoons had been treed by Ring, and their only escape was to work their way through the treetops to the water's edge and from there leap into the lake. They would be safe there. Ring wasn't one to leap into water.

Later, Ervin pointed out to me that beavers will slap their tails hard on the surface of the lake when annoyed. Ring had expanded the range of his job. I was delighted, not wanting beavers gnawing on my birches or poplars.

No, I certainly can't stand in judgment of Ring. He and I are friends again. It's that damned charm: paw on your knee, eyes refusing to leave yours until you show him love, so ingratiating with the breakfasts and sociability until we go onto mainland, where he's like my dad, underneath it all answerable only to himself. In and out of the water frequently now, he's eating more this year than ever before, actually interested in meals before they happen, even begging me for them, hopping up to do so. After meals he sleeps for a while on the porch on his back, back legs splayed, front ones tucked up on his chest; then he goes to make love to Blue for a while.

15

At first the return to warmer days was welcome, but now the sweltering heat is back. At 5:45 this morning the sun is a bright red ball on the horizon, reflecting a red path across the smooth lake and lighting the porch as though with red neon. Ms. Hummingbird sits patiently now, her slender black bill pointed east. Only occasionally does she come and go. She's been adding to her nest even as she broods, making it softer and deeper.

I spend much of the day in that alternate world with my mother. Heading back home, rounding the bend above Crow Lake, I see that far to the west the sky has darkened. It's been nothing but hazy sun for days, so that I've lost interest in weather reports, but now big, dark nimbus clouds are building towering monuments. I determine to outrace them and do quite well so long as I'm headed east on hard pavement, but turning south on the narrow, unpaved road I must slow down, watching the darkness move across the sky and wondering if I'll have to wait out a storm in the car. I'm not afraid of getting wet, but I don't want to be on the lake when lightning strikes. I think about the dogs, knowing they'll be terrified at the first clap of thunder.

When I get to my landing, I set out quickly, taking a chance, starting my motor with one pull, dragging the boat up to speed as fast as possible, thinking that I can pull in at Sugar Bush Point at the mouth of the bay if I need to get off the water. There's a sulfurous yellowness and stillness to the air and the sound of thunder not very far off. When I reach the point, a strong breeze lifts the surface into ragged waves, but I press on, sprayed by the waves as my bow hits them at an angle. The sky swells ahead of me, the thunderheads piling up, marked by flashes of lightning.

At the pass to the inner channel, thunder comes in surround

sound, but the lightning is still behind the Lewises' hill. Large
drops of rain punch the water and the wind comes in gusts, shov-
ing the bow of the boat this way and that. Facing forward to see
where I'm going feels like driving myself into a hail of bullets.
It seems to take longer than it ever has to run the channel to the
dock, and it's raining hard when I arrive and tie up, thunder shaking the world around me. I know I'm not safe until I get onto land,
and even then, lightning could strike the island.

Ring has heard me arrive and comes out from where he's
sought some cover from the roof overhang, timing it just right so
that he can scurry into the house with me without having to wait.
I strip off my wet shorts and shirt and towel myself dry, looking at
the downpour, so heavy the waves are flattened by it. The lightning
and thunder are almost simultaneous now, the cracks of thunder
thrilling. As always, I feel excitement rather than fear, and I don't
dwell on what my husband would have thought was my needless
recklessness. Over the years lightning has struck all the camps
around. Not long ago it burned down a sleeping cabin on Schoolmarm's Point. It struck my Hydro pole one year, knocking out my
power. The only place it hasn't struck is the Lewises' house on its
hill, the highest place around. I have a fire extinguisher on a rack.

Ring has taken refuge under the worktable in the kitchen. I
unplug the radio, the toaster, and an electric hot plate and go in to
put on dry clothes. No Blue. Calling her produces nothing, so I go
looking for her, finding her tucked way back under the log-framed
bed in the smaller bedroom. I ask her to come out, but she's trembling and won't move. I give up and watch the storm sweep past,
its fury sending rain horizontally under the roof overhang and
through the screens onto the porch, wetting the table and chairs. I
check on the hummingbird and see that she's flattened on the nest,
facing the wind. Inside the cabin there's water coming in where the
chimney meets the roof, bouncing off chimney stones and ancient
antlers, creating a fine spray that mists the room and dampens the
floor. The noise is tremendous.

And then it has moved to the east, all that electric current in
the air, leaving us with a steady dose of drumming rain still trying

to beat us into submission. The temperature has dropped twenty degrees Fahrenheit. Gradually the rain loses its intensity and the sounds of the tempest grow faint, but to the south and east lightning still flashes. I tell Ring it's OK now, but he doesn't believe me and stays under the table. I go to Blue and tell her it's all right with the same lack of success, but I stay with her for a while, talking and touching her trembling leg where I can reach it. We still hear thunder rolling eastward, *boooom boooom.*

The sun is free now to shine in on all the moisture. I know what that means and go to the dock, and there's the rainbow. Against the dark gun-metal grey clouds hovering over the eastern horizon a double arch, both bows with one foot in Mica Island, the other on Grape Island north of the pass, so vivid it does seem one could find their ends and stand showered with all that colored light. Suddenly everything is back: birdsong, boats, insects. The land is sodden, but the air is clear.

Ring joins me in the living room, but Blue still won't budge. She's able to get under that bed in a pinch, but she can't get out. I can pull her out, but only when she's ready to cooperate. I plug in the radio and listen to the Kingston weather report. It tells me belatedly that a front is bringing cooler air, seventy percent chance of a thunderstorm—then music, which I hope will help to calm Blue down.

I make buttered popcorn, a favorite of both dogs, and put some popped kernels down beside the bed. If anything will bring Blue out, food will. Several times she tries to crawl out, but each time she struggles, bangs her head, gives up and retreats, panting, into the corner. Finally, she gives herself up to me and I can slide her out on her side, popcorn her reward. Then we lose power. Brief intermittent pulses of light and sound from the radio; then it all goes dead.

The fickle moon will rise too late to help against darkness tonight. I bail the flooded boat and motor down to the place called Big Augur to see if the old couple that now own it have power, taking candles with me in case they need some. They don't have power, but I needn't have worried. They're outfitted with everything they need. I'm fond of them. When the Soviet space station Mir was launched in 1986, they read a schedule about finding it in the sky, came and got me, and we watched for it from their barge, which they called "Stargazer." Mir appeared out of the east and zipped across the sky at over 17,000 mph. A few years later I was again invited to recline on a deck chair on Stargazer, that time to watch a total lunar eclipse. Now Mir has been de-orbited, brought home to a fiery death in the earth's atmosphere after fifteen years in space, and the Stargazer is rotting on Big Augur's shores.

I decline their offer of a drink and head back to check my flashlights, eat what I can find without opening the refrigerator, and give the dogs canned dog food. Ring turns his back on it, so Blue eats it all. This end of the lake becomes as dark as it was before the Wilsons came and generated their own power, but tantalizingly, through the pass, I can see a light far to the north at Nordlaw Lodge. Inside, my candles light up little round areas of color and make the cabin look warmer than it feels. There are plenty of kerosene lamps to light if I want to bother, but in the end I get in bed and read by flashlight until I fall asleep.

At 5 a.m. the radio and lights come on, both dogs scared, shooting straight up wide-eyed.

16

There are mornings in the cabin, even in summer, when the lake seems to have been possessed by a different spirit, the air cold, wind whistling through the screens and whipping the Chinese wind chimes into a frenzy. Instead of blue water, the lake is grey, the islands hunched against the wind, the waves white-capped even in our channel, banging the boat against the dock or heaving it away to strain against its ropes. On days like these, the sounds of other lives are lost in the rush of air and water. Everything seems farther away, and few people venture out if they don't have to. Yet this is not when drownings occur. According to the stories I've heard, the lake captures people when they least expect it.

While I was young, a couple who had come to Nordlaw Lodge for years went out in their boat on a nice day with their five-year-old son. The woman, a strong swimmer, was riding on the prow of the boat in the main channel when something caused her to fall into the water. It's surmised that the boat and motor went over her and that the husband jumped into the water to save her. Both drowned. The child was found in the drifting boat, pointing to the water when asked where his parents were. Men dragged the lake looking for the bodies, but I'm not sure they were ever found.

On another occasion, a man was fishing in Mud Bay with his anchor down. Again, the day was lovely. When he decided to leave, he started his motor without drawing up the anchor. The boat roared off and was stopped short by the rope, throwing the man from the boat, which circled around the anchor until the tank ran out of gas, pulling him under in his self-created maelstrom.

A man transporting building materials by boat—from the landing at the Cedar Haven fishing camp—had his young grandson running the motor, while he himself sat forward on top of the load. As they rounded the point to turn toward his cottage, the man fell into the water. It might have been caused by a sudden motion of the boat or by some health-related problem. I was told that, instead of calling for help from the fishing camp, the boy left to get his grandmother. She found her husband dead in the water.

On a starry summer night, after visiting at Nordlaw, a family left and ran full throttle into the rock shoal which juts into the channel there, throwing people into the water, injuring some and drowning an elderly woman.

It was the year after my dad died when my mother and I felt the lake's hungry clutches. Knowing he was dying, my dad had recommended that she convert his office rooms in Kent into a small apartment, which she did, renting it to a newly married couple who were students at the university. We all became good friends, and we brought them with us to visit the cabin. I'm sure my mother thought it would be easier and safer for us to have them along.

The smaller and lighter of our two motorboats, the one my dad bought when he was dying so that we'd be able to handle it, and which I'm using now, was the one which we'd left in the garage. When we arrived in the evening with these new friends, we put everyone into it, including my cocker spaniel, Danny, along with a lot of heavy gear and groceries. With my mother running the motor, we set forth. Near the open mouth of the bay we encountered increasingly heavy waves, which would not have swamped our larger, 16-foot Peterborough boat, but in our inexperience we'd loaded this new boat far past its capacity, and it had no bow covering. Waves sloshed in bit by bit, lowering the boat even more, until the young woman in the front shouted, "The boat's sinking."

Several things happened at once. My mother began to turn back. I knew I could swim to shore and thought I could lighten the boat if I got out, so I dived over the side. That was a mistake, for when I came up, the boat was upside down and everyone was in the water. The burly young man with us had been wearing hip boots, which would have dragged him down had he not had the foresight to get one off and the other loosened before he went in.

At least the seats in that smaller boat are hollow molded fiberglass. You can't sink it, so everyone held onto it, surrounded by flotsam. There was a cottage overlooking this bay, and by chance a man and wife from Ithaca, New York, were there spending their last night before leaving for home, their motor off the boat and put away. Hearing us call, the man hurried to put it back on. Meanwhile, we wondered about my dog Danny, looking for his head among the floating gear and groceries, hoping he was swimming to shore. Before our rescuer arrived, my mother found Danny under the boat, drowned.

The man took us two at a time to shore, and his wife took us in and gave us dry clothes. Our woman friend was six months pregnant, and my mother called the well-named Dr. Goodfellow to come from Westport and make sure she was all right. The man from Ithaca scooped up as much of our floating gear as he could, righted and towed in our boat, and buried Danny there behind the cottage on the bay. We stayed there that night.

The next day, after having sat upside down in the lake, our motor would run only in reverse, trying to tell us something, I think. Our guests felt much the same way, and wouldn't have minded driving right back to Ohio without ever setting foot on the island, but my mother hired someone to take us across to the cabin. Once she'd settled our guests in, she took the motor to Westport to be worked on. Someone from down the lake with diving gear was thrilled to use it to retrieve nearly all our possessions, including handbags. We laid the money out on tables to dry, filled the clothesline with all manner of dripping things, and, for several years afterward, my family opened mystery cans without labels. In the end, our friends seemed to enjoy our big adventure. They were good sports, enjoyed fishing, and we had fun.

My mother blamed herself for not knowing the weight capacity of the boat. As far as I know, she never thought to blame my not infallible dad for buying us a bathtub of a boat with no bow covering. And I? If I hadn't dived overboard as she was turning, the boat probably would not have rolled, my dog would not have died, and we would not have baptized our friends in Bobs Lake. Plenty of blame to go around, but that was my mother's last visit to the lake for a long time. The island was mine, and the following year I brought my husband on our honeymoon, pointing out, I'm sure, to make him comfortable, that we'd capsized the boat the year before.

17

I set the ladder up by the back door where the porch roof is closest to the ground and carry up an open can of roof tar, a putty knife, and a broom. From the hill across the bay, I hear the *chug chug* of Ervin's haying machine. Long ago, before I was born, a wagon and team of horses disappeared into the depths of the lake through the ice. I recalled that terrible event a few years ago. I'd hired Ervin and another man to put this roof on my cabin after removing the old layer of shingles. They brought the new shingles on a barge across the water during the fall, but it was Ervin's intention to take the old ones off later by truck across the ice. At the end of March, he still hadn't done it, and by then on Long Island winter was over. I was sure all opportunity had passed, yet Ervin assured me that there was still ice and that he was going to do it. When I arrived in May, the old shingles were gone, the nails picked up by magnet, a good new roof was on, and somehow Ervin and his truck were still above ground.

The tall eastern hemlock near the kitchen corner is dying, like all eastern hemlocks these days, as the insect called woolly adelgid sucks the life out of it. I toss its fallen branches down from the roof and sweep off needle and leaf debris where it's collected over the gently sloping porch. The dogs lie down below, unconcerned. Elsewhere, Blue barks with alarm at people on roofs or workers high on utility poles, but now that I'm the one teetering around up in the air, she pays no attention at all. She expects anything from me.

When I climb onto the steeper part to inspect the joint between rock chimney and roof at the peak, I find that large cracks have formed in the black caulking. It's no wonder the heavy rain streamed through. It's fun to fill them, poking the tar down into the cracks, then smoothing it over. The tar has warmed in the sun to the consistency of chocolate frosting.

While I'm working there, a belted kingfisher alights below me in the big birch tree behind the cabin, a baby sunfish in its beak. I'm arrested by the sight, while the kingfisher has no idea I'm perched on the peak of the roof, observing it. The kingfisher's tall, forward-swept crest, thick neck, and oversized bill make its head seem too big for its body. The little sunfish is round and bright yellow, too small to struggle in the stout bill. The picture strikes me as pretty, the blue bird with the small yellow fish, but as the kingfisher moves on, perhaps to feed its mate and young in a hillside tunnel they've burrowed, I wonder why some scenes of nature have that kind of instant appeal to us humans and not others. Why does this scene seem to me *cute*? Human aesthetics can seem capricious. Kingfishers eat their fish alive, after all, but when wolves work together socially to bring down a deer to feed themselves, humans are unlikely to think of it as cute. They'll often sympathize with the deer, in spite of the fact that humans hunt deer with the help of their beloved canines.

When I'm satisfied that the roof will no longer leak, I throw down the putty knife and broom and carry the tar down the ladder, glad to feel flat ground under my feet. Paint thinner removes the tar from my fingers and the putty knife, and I hammer the lid back on the old tar can and store it in the boathouse to be used for years to come.

At the back dock, a gentle breeze flutters the silvery leaves of the silver maple trees. Mallards like this backwater, feeding along the shore among spatterdock and smartweed, and the dogs watch them carefully. Blue strides into the water but I ask her not to cross the lagoon and she obeys. She's used to indulging what she regards as my unreasonable concern for ducks and mergansers. Ring knows the folly of floundering in the water to try to catch a duck.

The mother duck leads her seven ducklings farther along the peninsula. This mother must be vigilant against predators from above and below. There are eagles that nest at the southern end of Bobs Lake, and eagles are fond of ducklings. So are snapping turtles. The most dangerous threat to ducks comes in the fall, of course, when these little ones have grown. I never ate a duck shot by my father, but that's what he and his friends hunted and ate. Men, guns, and alcohol. That's what it takes. Laura Lee Davidson titled her second book about this lake *Isles of Eden.* If Eden is a place where living things kill and are killed, I'm in Eden.

I wonder how anyone could bear to pluck and eat a gorgeous wood duck drake. The meat, I'm sure, tastes the same as that of the common mallard, and yet, I suppose they were considered a real prize. Ervin has one stuffed and displayed on his television, but I've never seen a stuffed squirrel! The more beautiful the prey, the more sought after to be killed.

I know that to survive on the land requires a different code than that adopted by the city-dweller. Hughie and Ervin naturally hunted and set traps to put food on the table. In terms of the reduction of wildlife on this continent, the cutting of the prime forest in the nineteenth century may ultimately have done more to diminish wildlife numbers than hunters and trappers did. They weren't more rapacious than the bulldozer that precedes the suburbanite, and the pain of the hunt or trap may not be worse than some of the life-long degradation imposed upon animals in raising meat for our supermarkets. We humans have industrialized the killing of what we eat, fooling ourselves into thinking we are not the ones who draw the knife along the throat.

I haven't always had this back dock. My daughter Molly's husband has left his mark on the island. After college Molly sought her fortune in Northern California. When she told us she'd found someone to marry, she said that if there were only one other person on earth besides herself, she would want it to be Chris Morris, because he could do anything. When she next returned to the island, we understood. Her husband, Chris, took one look at the poplar-log boathouse rotting into the lake and asked me, "Do you have a railroad jack?"

By the time he left ten days later, he'd borrowed tools from Ervin, turned our boat trailer into a hauling bed, raised the lake end of the boathouse onto a cement footer with twenty-one bags of cement and some rock, and two heights of railroad tie. He'd mended or replaced the boathouse doors and windows, brought one boatload of huge rocks to protect the shore, sailed our Sunfish, and caught walleyes with Ervin and Carl, the fisherman. Chris said he'd never played Hearts before, but when dealt his first hand, he Shot the Moon.

The following year, using forty-five bags of cement and railroad ties, he set the other end of the boathouse on its footer, dug out the rotten floor, installed a new one supported on pier blocks, and rebuilt and shingled the roof.

Now, I don't mean he did this all alone. He organized the whole family into work parties. That's the special genius of Chris. He devised ways of moving us to move the earth, towing our dock around to Lewis Bay near a hill on the farm, hauling dirt in wheelbarrows from the hill onto the dock, dumping it into the fiberglass boat tied to the dock, towing the boat over and over again to the island, and shoveling dirt around the boathouse to make it high and dry. The pace he sets is merciless. Even the dogs become infected with hysterical activity, Blue in the water, Ring worrying onshore. Chris put Blue to work pulling the boat to shore by its rope and she set her legs and pulled with all her might. In addition, Chris caught fish suppers for us, refitted the cabin doors, built a back stoop, and was frustrated because he had ideas for doing things he couldn't fit into three weeks. And he beat us all at Scrabble.

Possession is more than a name on a deed. It means carrying the idea of the place with you when you leave, and planning all year for it as my father did. When Chris did return, he'd designed and bought materials for this back dock that he and my son, James, assembled on Ervin's hill and slid into the lake. The trouble is that Molly and Chris live on the west coast, have children and busy lives there now, and seldom get to Bobs Lake. Chris had the desire and ability to possess the place. James, however, has always had possession of it in his heart, just as I do, without having known what a railroad jack is.

Chris thanking the dogs
for a job well done

18

Joan comes to visit. I pick her up at the landing at the entrance to Mud Bay where the Lewises have always left their car. She's brought me fresh whole-wheat bread from the bakery in Sharbot Lake, and I make sandwiches with canned chicken, lettuce, and tomato. Then we sit on the porch and rock awhile. She's not interested in going over to the farm. It's Ervin's now. Anyway, we don't need to go there. We're there in our minds while we reminisce about the old days.

My friendship with Joan was honed during a long string of summers. We learned to swim together along the island's shore. As soon as I was old enough to row a boat, I'd head for her house, sometimes even before she was awake in the morning. I must have been a pest. We might follow her mother, Lizzie, to pick thimble berries in the old horse pasture or tangle ourselves up in a hammock strung between apple trees. The summer farm was hot, the soil and stubble of cut hay near the house dry and full of grasshoppers. The apple trees were hung like Christmas trees, the apples a tempting size but still green, the upper pastures humming with the drone of flies and the buzz of cicadas, and all around, the lake blue with silver sparkles.

The farm dogs sprawled inside the house during the afternoons, a few porcupine quills in their muzzles. Joan and I often played cards. If it rained and we tired of the games, we could look through the thick Eaton's catalogue, the Canadian equivalent of Sears in those days. The boys would come in from the field and rest by the radio, tapping their feet and rolling their own cigarettes with Hogden's tobacco. When Joan's cousins came to spend time on the farm, I played with them too. The Lewises felt like an extension of my own small family.

Joan Lewis, left, and the author

Joan never complains about her life, though compared to mine it has been hard. She attended a one-room school in nearby Crow Lake, taught by a woman from Toronto named Effie Milne Bedore. Effie Milne had gotten the job directly after finishing her own schooling. Driving her into this back country, her father gave her two weeks before he figured he'd have to come and get her. Instead, Effie stayed and married a man named Hilliard Bedore who lived on the shores of Bobs Lake and ran a lumber mill. Joan rode to school with Effie every day, at first in a buggy, with a horse supplied by her dad, Hugh Lewis. Later they went by car, but Joan says Effie was a poor driver. Joan would sometimes have to walk back to ask Hilliard to come and dig them out of a snowbank. Effie taught at Crow Lake for twenty-five years until the school closed in 1963.

When Joan had completed eight grades, she boarded with an uncle's family in Sharbot Lake to attend high school, returning to the farm during the summers. A nephew of Hilliard's delivered something to the Lewises' while she was there, and it wasn't long before Joan became Mrs. Keith Bedore. After they were married, Keith had a job lining pipes with asbestos in Kingston. Their first child was born, a daughter. Then something happened that changed their lives. She told me the story years ago.

One evening, driving home from work, for some reason he couldn't later remember, Keith swerved on Highway 38, taking out fourteen posts on a guard rail and plummeting over a bank. He was thrown thirty feet from the car into a small tree and shallow water. His left arm was severed, his jaw broken, his face around his eyes battered, one ankle crushed and that leg badly gashed. A passerby put a tourniquet on the arm to stop the loss of arterial blood, but then left and drove on. Joan has no idea who that might have been, but is certain it saved Keith's life.

In a photograph of the car taken afterward, I could see that it was totally smashed, wrenched, all its doors twisted full open. Keith was operated on all night and given a thirty percent chance to live. Joan said that in the hospital they were just amazed at him. They thought that because he was an outdoorsman, he'd survived the exposure in water while in shock without getting pneumonia. They didn't think he'd ever walk on the ankle again and almost amputated it. Instead, they just shoved the crushed bone back and put on a cast.

For two or three days his head was swollen double and black. They saved his eyes and wired shut his broken jaw, leaving him able to consume only liquids. He lost forty pounds. Yet, he was so anxious to get home that he insisted on leaving the hospital after three weeks. They wouldn't give him crutches because he had no left arm and a cast on his left leg, so they let him go, at his insistence, but put him in a wheelchair. The agreement was that he had to return to Kingston every Wednesday as an outpatient. The next Wednesday he went in there on a crutch!

In October he told the plastic surgeon who repaired his face that he was going deer hunting. The doctor winked at Joan and said, "Bring me some venison." Keith's friends took him deer hunting, left him at a blind, and he shot a deer. The doctor got his venison and sent a card at Christmas with the part of the bill not covered by insurance marked "Paid in Full."

Keith's friends were very good at helping him rebuild his life, but there were trials. One photograph of that time shows him on Christmas Eve trying to assemble the parts of a doll's carriage with one hand. Joan said that gave him quite a time. "Did you help him?" I asked. "Oh no! He was determined, and he did it."

Somehow his ankle healed. When he was once again able to work, he became a painter, up on tall ladders painting the outside walls of houses. And, Joan said, his two-armed partner would work on the lower part of the house while Keith, with one arm, was always by choice at the top. Eventually the Bedores bought their house in Sharbot Lake and had a second daughter.

For a while it seemed Keith had overcome the worst life could offer, but then he was diagnosed with lung cancer. He investigated and found that every man he had worked with in laying asbestos was either dead or dying of the same thing. This time no amount of courage could save him.

No class action suit has been pursued to compensate Joan for the loss of her husband. She's been a widow for fifteen years and is very busy with several jobs. Her daughters and their husbands are a source of help and companionship. She and I still celebrate her birthday together every August.

Joan at the cabin

Late this afternoon on the way back to her car, we stop at Cedar Haven Camp to walk the familiar dusty road up to the rural-route mail boxes where the Lewises have always received their mail. It follows along the shore of the lake and passes a tiny Anglican church. Long ago, Laura Lee Davidson, an Episcopalian, decided that a place of worship was needed on the lake and garnered support for building one. Its bell still occasionally announces a worship service on summer Sunday afternoons. Laura Lee published her third book, *We Build*, to describe the community effort and the church's dedication in grand style by the Bishop of Ontario, who arrived with choir and entourage in a flotilla of boats. Laura Lee named it St. Andrew's, after "the first fisherman to follow Our Lord."

By chance we find someone coming out of the church. They've been cleaning and are about to lock up. We ask if we may look inside. Simple yet beautiful, with pews to seat forty and kerosene lanterns for lighting, it's an antique treasure.

* * *

Ring has many burrs stuck in his long fine hair this evening, and together he and I sit on a grassy knoll as I try to work them out. He prefers to do it himself with his teeth, so I pretend I'm just petting him, murmuring sweet nothings as I pull the hairs apart behind his ears where he can't reach to loosen the burrs' grip. If I become too serious, he'll put his teeth on my hand without biting.

Things *plip* and *plop* in the water, sending concentric circles along the otherwise smooth surface. We hear the distant motor of Ervin's runabout tractor and Ring stares home intently. An osprey circles Lewis Bay, diving once in a while with a violence oddly in keeping with the otherwise tranquil mood, nearly disappearing below the surface before rising, its wings beating and taking off effortlessly because it's empty-clawed. From the nest on Goose Island, two chicks watch closely, demanding more success with their plaintive cries.

Ring looking home

19

Today is the hottest one yet. Occasionally isolated swollen thunderheads roll randomly through, none a cooling front, and so far no more rain has fallen here. That's enabled Ervin, with Carl the fisherman's help, to store in his barn four hundred bales of green oats, planted to be cut for hay unripened before the stalks become straw.

It's a day for driving to Sharbot Lake. At the garage, as I'm changing from island shoes into sandals, I see two cows coming down the drive, clearly wanting to cool off in the lake. They aren't supposed to be here. The last thing I want at the landing are cow pies and mud wallows. *Shoo* I tell them, waving my arms as I rush at them, one shoe on, one shoe off, telling them in no uncertain terms that they can't come down. They believe me and turn back up the drive, but before I get into the driver's seat, I hear them crashing through brush farther south in order to get to the swamp. I have to laugh, but when I drive up to the road, I see they've gone through a farmhouse garden filled with zinnias, cosmos, and some good tomatoes.

When I get to the Seniors Home, I'm shocked. Dorothea looks gray, almost like a corpse. They have her in a Geri Chair in the parlor covered with a blanket, while the staff in the Home all have bright red faces from the heat as they move about the house. They don't bother taking her to the table for meals anymore but merely try to keep her sipping Ensure. I rub some cream into the dry and brittle skin of her hands. She opens her eyes but closes them with no sign of recognition. I'll begin coming every other day now.

After lunchtime, one of the residents is pounding out hymns on the piano in the parlor, too fast for anyone to sing along. She doesn't hold out the whole notes where people would naturally breathe before starting a new phrase, probably because she herself doesn't sing. In fact, she rarely talks. No one ever asks her to change the pace of her playing, so the audience tries to grab a word here, a phrase there, as the tune rushes by. A perfunctory *Amazing Grace*, a raucous *Softly and Tenderly*, a galloping *Silent Night*. In spite of this, Dorothea's still asleep in her recliner chair, and nothing I say or do keeps her awake, so we decide to let her nap there rather than move her to bed. Meanwhile, I go instead to visit Joan's mother, Lizzie, in her apartment near Joan's house.

It takes Lizzie a long time to get to the door today, but she greets me in a sweet motherly way, unlike my mother, with full knowledge of who I am and what we've been to one another. Using her walker, she leads the way to the small living room. On the table next to the couch where we sit is a well-worn photo album, and together, we look at our pasts. Talking of old times brings us both a mixture of pleasure and sadness.

Today, for the first time, she talks about having had a miserable existence. I've known Lizzie all my life, but I've never had a woman-to-woman talk with her before. I knew that her father, Richard McVeigh, was a Scot and worked for the railroad; her mother, Julia Bain, of Irish descent, was from Crow Lake and was deaf from Scarlet Fever. Lizzie'd had enough education to read and write, but the only jobs available to her were as what the British call a "skivvy." She tells me that she met Hughie at a house dance in Crow Lake where he was the fiddler. He hired her to help his mother, Harriet, with chores on the farm. After a time, when Hughie proposed marriage, she now confides to me that she'd had no choice, nowhere else to go. At the time, she was seventeen. Hughie was forty-three.

I knew Lizzie's life working for old Mrs. Lewis had been hard, and even after the death of her mother-in-law, she would never have felt the same sense of ownership. It was a sort of lifelong indenture. It was a dairy farm then, and I remember her carrying large milk pails up along the ridge to the house after milking twice a day, her ankles swollen even as a young woman. She'd have to pasteurize, then separate cream from milk in an old centrifuge and churn the cream for butter, tend her garden, cook on a wood stove, bake bread, haul the water up from the well in the basement, and care for the children.

She says things became a little easier for her when they got electricity in the 1950s, when Joan and I were becoming teenagers. Flipping a switch to turn darkness to light saved all the effort and risk involved in using coal oil lamps. We recall how Keith, her older son, found a used electric stove for her, but, as he was crossing the lake with it on a barge, waves caused it to fall off and disappear into the depths. The same man with diving equipment who brought our belongings up out of the bay went down and hooked a rope onto the stove. What a day on the lake! There was a crowd cheering from boats around the barge as Keith and the other man hauled it up, gushing water from its interior. They got it uphill to the house, dried it out, plugged it in, and Lizzie cooked on it for years. And later, the addition of a free-standing freezer was a great boon, allowing the family to freeze and store fish, venison, and beef from cattle they raised.

Lizzie seldom went anywhere. She never ventured onto the lake, couldn't swim, and feared the children would drown. Her relatives would come with their children for vacations in the country and Lizzie's work would be increased. Her children encouraged Lizzie to learn to drive, but in spite of her isolation, she resisted. Knowing how much it would enhance her life, Ervin tried to shame his mother into driving, calling her a coward. "Be a lot of dead people," was her reply. She was ever fearful, the nervous type.

Hughie's sense of humor sometimes depended upon misogyny. My dad used to love to tell the story about the day Lizzie's father died and she was going to Sharbot Lake for the funeral. Hughie was on our island sitting at the breakfast table with my parents, and my mother expressed sadness for Lizzie. Yes, Hughie agreed. To show his sympathy he'd milked a cow for her that morning.

"Only one cow, Hughie?" my father asked. "Why didn't you milk them all?"

"Oh no," Hughie said quickly. "Nah, tha' twould spile 'er."

My dad would laugh and laugh about that.

Hughie lived to ninety-five and, when he died of pneumonia, Lizzie signed the farm over to Ervin. Now in old age, Lizzie suffers terribly from arthritis and has trouble bending her knees.

I think there must be strength in such endurance, to overcome a long, tedious, unrewarded life and remain so sweet and unresentful.

Ervin and Lizzie in the summer kitchen

20

A cooler day! Eating lunch on the porch, I think I hear a bumblebee but it's the hummingbird. She's coming and going busily again, so she must have someone in that nest to feed. I take the dogs for a long walk from the garage up the narrow road through woods and meadows full of wildflowers. Back at the landing, Blue goes straight into the lake, while Ring lies panting nearby as I rake last year's leaves away from Ervin's garage and mine. When there are six large leaf bags in the boat, the dogs pile in among them, and we motor back to the island. The leaves, released from the black plastic, fall in damp clumps behind the wall, and I'm free to sit on the front dock with my feet cooling in the water, thinking about my dad. He never swam in the lake, just bathed here beside the dock. Now that I think about it, I suspect he may not have been as at home here as I am, much as he loved this place and wanted to be. His was a more confrontational approach to nature.

The year he died, he'd made his annual spring trip here to fish, this time with our postman, Al Peoples. In retrospect my parents realized my dad had not been well, but my mother couldn't persuade him not to go. He was short of breath and had trouble walking up the slightest incline, signs which they attributed to a lifetime of smoking Kool cigarettes. He was trying to "cut down." During the second night on the island with Al, Phil was stricken with a hemorrhaging ulcer, vomiting blood outside in the dark, not knowing what it was. At first light, when he saw that it was blood, he awakened Al and sent him to the Lewises, who called Dr. Goodfellow in Westport. When the doctor arrived at the garage and saw my dad, he drove him the fifty miles to the Kingston hospital himself, barely in time to save his life. They gave him transfusions, pumped his stomach, and stopped the bleeding.

When Al arrived back in Kent in my parents' car, my mother, not knowing whether she would find her husband alive or dead, drove to Kingston and found him weak but very glad to see her. Within a week my dad was released, with the news that they'd found he had an abdominal aneurysm the size of a grapefruit and would surely die soon if he didn't seek the help of a new technique for repairing the artery with nylon tubing.

He was only sixty-five, but his first impulse was not to try to save himself. When he'd decided in 1918 to study chiropractic, it was a faith-based creed unrecognized by the American Medical Association, which fought hard to prevent the licensing of chiropractic practitioners. Phil had built his practice upon the "straight method," relying solely on spinal adjustments, and was never challenged, but he felt embattled by the medical profession. It took a month before my mother was able to convince him to go to the veterans' hospital in Cleveland.

It took the doctors another month to get Phil into shape to operate. Already weakened by the ulcer, his situation was complicated by arteriosclerosis and emphysema. When they thought they could safely proceed, they found that the aneurysm involved both arteries to the kidneys and was too extensive for them to repair. They sewed him up again, guessing he could live a day, a month, maybe more. This time it was reported that with each heartbeat, the aneurysm ballooned to football size. They thought when it went, it would be sudden, but at his insistence they discharged him. What he chose to do with his last days was to return to the island.

I had spent the summer with a friend, working at a Girl Scout camp on the Potomac River in Virginia. Still a teenager, I was aware that my father was gravely ill and might die, but it hadn't seemed very real to me until I received a phone call from my mother. He was being released, and it was time for me to fly home. I grabbed my high school boyfriend to do the heavy lifting, and my mother drove us all to Bobs Lake.

For ten days in Canada the weather was beautiful, my boyfriend was good company, and we had a pretty good time—in spite of our fear that my dad would die while we were there. Within a week of our return to Kent, my dad was back in the hospital, slowly bleeding to death. After twenty-four hours, when his heart finally stopped beating, it had become very real. It was happening to me! Thinking at the time that I should spare her *my* anguish, I left my mother alone and ran out of the ward. In a stairwell, I crumpled as though I'd been shot. *"My father's dead! My father's dead."*

My mother planned a funeral conducted by all three Protestant minister friends who'd been to the island. Weeping inconsolably, we buried him on a Saturday, his coffin draped with a veteran's flag, and I felt my heart had been broken. But on the following Monday, I entered Kent State University as a freshman. I lived at home, got straight A's, joined a sorority, went to Europe for two months the following summer, and felt I could swallow the world whole.

My mother found a job right away, working in the university registrar's office. Oddly, I felt in charge, solicitous about my mother, but exactly two years after my father died, I married and moved away. Soon afterward, she returned to her pre-marital profession, teaching music in public schools. He'd had a life insurance policy that paid her only $100 per month. She moved into a smaller house, jettisoning furniture and other familiar objects of our former life.

The island was all I had left of my father. My dad had spoken often to me about its being mine one day. Because it was decided that I should inherit it directly, I assumed ownership at seventeen with all the presumption of youth, while my mother still paid the bills. With her decision to let it go so easily, I began to see how different she was from him. And from me. I felt he was the one upon whom I must model myself, whose passions would be my passions, whose memory I would revere. He and the island slid into my mind as one. It was here to return to, year after year, while he wasn't.

I don't recall ever admiring my mother's courage and determination in guiding my coming of age while facing loneliness as a widow. I guess I'd perceived a weakness in my mother that, as a teenager, I didn't expect from a parent. I grew to think that, in her relationship with her husband, she was guilty of appeasement. She'd never complained, always a pleaser. She called him "boss." Wouldn't things have been better if she had drawn a few lines in the sand? In the domestic scene created by addictions and illness, I must have felt betrayed by a mother who was powerless to stop the shaking of the foundation of our lives. The passing of a parent when you're young is an earthquake, tilting you off balance. I've been standing on ground raised by such an upheaval over forty years ago, and this summer I realize I'm feeling the first seismic spasms as the fault line readjusts.

My father always commanded so much of my attention that I've neglected to see that my mother probably did much more to empower me than my dad did. She let me go my own way, but was always there when I needed her, trusting me to make my own decisions, sending me on the tour of Europe the first summer after my dad died while she labored at an unfamiliar job to make ends meet. I'm embarrassed now to remember how I always took her for granted. I was too selfish to have imagined that she could

have let me inherit the island as an act of love. I've never thought of myself as a spoiled only child, but there it is. She'd taken care of her own aged mother and knew she didn't want to cause me an early visit to the inhospitable landscape of the old, so she made an independent life for herself a continent away.

The author young and in charge

21

They've stopped getting Dorothea up at all and have put her in a hospital gown. The doctor has said it won't be long, so it's a death watch now. She doesn't respond to voice or touch and can't swallow well. I spend much of the day in her room. I take her hand and she seems to clutch it, but her movements are spasmodic.

A staff member named Beth teaches me how to help pull and roll my mom's body using a sheet folded under her to keep the blood from pooling under the skin and causing bedsores. Seeing my mother's legs now, I'm reminded that the German word for legs is *beine*, bones. That's all her long legs are now, just bones, a sharp white line of a shin, the femur outlined, and there's no flesh on her hips or belly.

Beth uses a dropper to place water and small amounts of liquid Tylenol on the back of my mom's tongue. While her breath smells like the grave, her white hair is still glorious. The director has promised me that they will give her morphine if she's in pain, but she slept quietly almost all day after we got Tylenol into her. Poor Mother. It's long and drawn out to the end.

Back on my island, I try to block all that out, forget it. I turn on the radio loudly while I boil macaroni and dice local aged cheddar, but I find myself talking to Blue about "Grandma," admitting that she's dying. With the mac and cheese in the oven, I head for the chair on the back dock. The sun is low above the hill where Ervin and June are sitting out under the apple tree. Joan telephones them every day about what's happening, and they watch for my boat every evening to make sure I've made it home.

The next morning, I wake to lots of leaf noise and the boat slapping water and scraping the buffers on the dock, a symphony of splashes and squeaks. Wind whistles along the front screens and plays music in the wind chimes, which, while lovely, is just part of the hullabaloo. The red rocking chair on the porch rocks by itself.

Hoping the wind will drop, I let Blue out, then both dogs in. The hummingbird is flattened on the nest, facing the wind. I return to bed for an hour, only to find that, if anything, the wind has become even more determined. It's as though nature outside the cabin was suddenly taken up with something important beyond my understanding and is ignoring me. I feel like a child at an adult party, amid a roar of activity that I observe but don't feel part of. And yet, I see a little song sparrow hunting among the leaves on the ground, seemingly unaffected by the weather.

Blue seems jumpy . . . and especially hungry. So am I. So much wind makes life seem like work. I dress warmly (my thermometer reads sixty degrees), make a batch of pancakes, three for me with syrup and one each plain for the dogs, and eat inside out of the wind, then motor over to the Lewises and call the Seniors Home on their land phone. Dorothea's had a quiet night and one of the staff gave her Tylenol this morning.

When I've washed the dishes, the wind is still heavy, gusting from the north, but I have no choice. I must make the crossing. Since Blue will be locked in the house all day, I set water and some dog food in the kitchen for her to eat later. Of course, she eats the food immediately. If she weren't so aggressive, I might ask someone to come and let her out while I'm gone, but she would undoubtedly threaten them and then set out swimming to the garage. Just as I'm fastening on a life vest with every belt and buckle, Carl, the fisherman, comes to give me fillets of a bass and a walleye he's caught. I thank him and put them in the refrigerator. When I take off a few minutes after he does, I see that he's gone around the south end of Mica Island and is now sitting in the main channel where he can see me crossing the hazardous waves in my small boat until I turn into the bay toward my garage.

Today my mother is much the same as yesterday, propped on

one side with pillows. I take her hand, and, again, she grips mine with spasmodic movements. When Beth comes in, I ask her about it, thinking my mom must be in pain. She explains that the clutching is involuntary, a symptom of the throes of death. There are signs of the blood pooling under her skin, and we turn her frequently.

Each day while I'm in Sharbot Lake, my son James talks to me. His instinct is that he's needed, and he thought he should come to Sharbot Lake, but I discouraged him. He lives in Manhattan and has no car. As a photo news editor, he would find it hard to be away from his job, and renting a car would mean two days for travel alone. Air travel also would be complicated, considering where I am. Today he's standing in Central Park while I'm stroking her head, and I tell him it won't be long now. I assure him that he came through when he *was* needed. While his Grandma lived with us in New York and needed a friend, James was the one she could talk to. He helped me in many ways then. He's made several trips here to visit her at the Home, finding ways to entertain her. James always had a special understanding of the needs of older people, but now she wouldn't know he was here, and there isn't any great reason for him to see her die.

I talk to Molly as well. She's concerned about me also, but she's pragmatic, knowing there's no point to her leaving her job and family and crossing the continent. She, too, can keep her grandmother through memories of better times. It helps me just to talk to her.

Such is my relationship with my husband that it would never occur to either of us that he should come to be with me. I can reach him more often now that I'm in Sharbot Lake daily. He knows my mother's death will be a relief to me. It's another step in the long process that was my concern, not his. He's used to my dealing with things on my own.

At three o'clock in the afternoon, I go upstairs in the Home to a guest shower and wash my hair, a luxury compared to sponge bathing in the cabin in this chilly weather. Joan picks me up to take me to a fund-raising supper at a nearby church. We walk into a hall filled with the smell of roasting turkeys and hams. After we've eaten at one of the long, paper-covered tables, I hurry back to check on Mother one more time—no change—before driving back to the kingdom of the North Wind.

On the lake the wind seems even busier than it was in the morning, sweeping into the bay with momentum gathered on the long reach from the north. The boat's been driven up onto the small dock by the garage. I retrieve it, but it's hard to row out against the waves far enough to start my motor. By sheltering in the lee of a boathouse built at the end of a long nearby pier, I can uncock the motor and pull the rope. Heading out of the bay, I'm sprayed with water each time I buck a wave. Crossing the main channel, I have to go off course to the northwest in order to quarter the waves enough to keep from being side-swamped. I round Grape Island, then shoot south down the somewhat calmer inner channel with the wind behind me. It's nearly dark when I get home. I feed the dogs, then take Ring back to the Lewises'. Leaving him on the chain, I crank the motor and roar home, trying to drown out his pleading voice, which follows me down the hill and across the water.

I'm asleep by ten.

At 3 a.m. I awaken and sit up, thinking I've heard my mother's voice calling me. It's as though someone has just hit my emotional switch. It was stupid not to stay in Sharbot Lake overnight. Why did I come back here? Determined as always to get away, to separate the sadness from me, but I can't divide myself in two anymore. The wind has died and I leave at first light, taking Blue and an overnight bag with me. Blue will just have to hang out in the car.

A doe and spotted fawn are grazing near the road in the pre-dawn light as I leave the lake. At first they run ahead of me on the road, then off in separate directions. The fawn is confused but does what is sensible. It looks at me and then goes a little farther off the road to wait. Blue gives an incredulous *woof*. Further on the dirt road I wait while a fat porcupine waddles himself into the side weeds, but otherwise I see no one about until I get to the Home at 6:15.

I'm relieved to find my mother alive, glad to confirm that my middle-of-the-night dream wasn't some final goodbye. Whatever transcendental message came to me originated in my own brain. I called myself to duty. The night nurse is there and we turn my mom's body slightly, propping her at a new angle. Her breathing is ragged, her nails dark, and her limbs are moving even more spasmodically this morning. The apparent discomfort is hard to watch, and I ask if we can give her morphine.

The director comes with it and releases one-half teaspoon in small drips on my mom's tongue, waiting after each drip while she struggles to swallow, then steps out.

"Mother, I think you're going to die now," I say softly. I hold one of her hands firmly in my two. "You were a wonderful mother to me." There's no sign that she can hear or understand me. While I have no orthodox explanations for what happens to us when we die, I'm suddenly a good child and speak her language. "God will take you to Him. You'll be with God soon." Of course, I've always known that religion can be comforting if you believe, but it never crossed my mind that *I*, a disbeliever now, would find comfort from having these words to say.

Rituals are needed as a structure for the emotions we feel at momentous times. Just as my grandmother was sure she would see Sam in the "next life," my mother also looked forward to death, though I don't know that she believed she'd be united with a husband, and *which* husband she'd want to be reunited with was a question I don't want to think about. I just tell her that she deserves God's love, and then I have to stop. I'm making myself cry.

The sun streams over Sharbot lake and across the room, and the house comes to life, residents passing in the hall to go to breakfast, the smell of bacon in the air. My mom's breathing is very hesitant now. The director comes back and we sit on opposite sides of the bed. She asks me to tell her about Dorothea's life. At 8:15 I'm holding my mother's hand, pausing to wonder if I should go out and relieve Blue for a minute, when the director suddenly rises and says, "I think she's gone now." And indeed she has. She's gone. I sob out of pity for her and out of relief.

My mother always said she wanted to be cremated. Once I've signed over her body to Goodfellows' Funeral Home, I leave the Seniors Home and talk to my children, then my husband. This time I insist that he come to the phone and wait for his secretary to locate him. He's out of the building. I ask her to find him and have him call me back. It's an emergency. I head off with Blue for a walk by Sharbot Lake.

My phone rings. "What's up?"

"My mother died this morning."

"Well, you've been expecting this to happen. Now it will be easier for you."

He's right. My life will be easier. I tell him some of the details briefly, aware that he needs to get on with whatever he's doing.

Blue brings me a stick and I hang up and throw the stick into the water. I can't throw it far enough for her, hauling back and letting go over and over. Each time she plunges after it and returns to shake and bark for another throw, I feel a bit of release. When I go back to the Home to say goodbye and thank the staff, Beth gives me a small pin shaped like an angel to keep me safe.

So, my mother is dead at ninety-seven. Her muddled mind had effectively cut her off from life and friends for years. I threw a big party years ago in my house on her ninetieth birthday, inviting all those who had in some way been kind to us while she was living with me. Her niece came from upstate New York, bringing her son. I made a large poster with photos showing my mom at different times in her life, and ordered a cake with musical notes and her name on it. After dinner she and I sang a duet, and then everyone sang Dorothea's old favorites from sheets I'd prepared, while two pianist friends took turns accompanying us. My mother loved the attention.

The party wound down, just a few people still with us watching TV where a white Bronco was driving down a California freeway. I asked, 'Who's O.J. Simpson?' Dorothea went to her room but came out again to thank me for the party. We said goodnight again, but she came out twice more to thank me. The next day she had no recollection at all of the night before, and I believe that she'd probably realized that she would forget and wanted to be sure she gave me her thanks. I think of that as her funeral. She had a good time.

Blue is content now to sleep in the car while I spend time with Joan at her house, making some lunch and talking about our mothers. Because Lizzie grows more and more helpless, soon she, too, will be in the Seniors Home. And when, we wonder, will it be our turn? At the filling station up on the highway, I feel something close to joy as I unscrew the fuel tank cap, realizing that I won't be burning through so much gas now, won't be spending so much time on the road, then realize I'm not supposed to feel this way. What happened to the grief? Well, I've seen it through now. As usual, I will just go on. Blue and I head home to Ring.

It's one of those crisp blue, white, and green summer after-noons on the lake, two sailboats tacking like gulls down the main channel. On the crossing to the Lewises', my cap blows off in the breeze and I have to circle back to pick it out of the water before it sinks. Receiving hugs from Ervin and June, I feel like a fake. They think I must be sad but instead I feel light enough to walk across the bay.

Home again, both dogs scramble to secure the perimeter, nos-es to the ground. I pour myself a glass of wine and drink enough to feel a little deeper in my bones while I dip Carl's fish in beaten egg, then breadcrumbs, and fry them. Walleyes are highly valued, but I like smallmouth bass just as well and eat them both gratefully, saving half for later. A generous gift.

Afraid of bones in the fish for the dogs, I mix some leftover mac and cheese in their kibble and they're happy. When the dishes are washed, I sit in the red rocking chair on the porch. I've been expecting my mother's death for years, but now I feel that aware-ness, common after the loss of the last parent, that the interceding figure is gone and you're next. There was always that one above you who's suddenly no longer there. It's like someone removing the roof on your house. You feel exposed.

On the radio, a recording of right whales and killer whales off the coast of Antarctica. Their voices are varied and mimetic, often too low for us humans to hear, paced according to a long, slow rhythm. They may skip a beat but come back in sync, perhaps eight minutes apart. Their sense of time and space—they can hear each other clearly over several hundred miles!—is different from ours, and they live twice as long as we do. Hearing them somehow consoles me. When the program ends, I turn the radio off.

High cumulus clouds mirror the last sunlight onto the water. A fishing boat, a Tracker, pulls in at the bass hole by Bear Island. Its wake makes its splashy way along the opposite shore, then chugs more slowly around me. Then quiet again, and the heron glides in to land on the point of Goose Island on the chance the fisherman will catch something too small to keep and toss it. The boat is close to shore and the heron gets as close as he can. What a panhandler!

A crow over at the Lewises' is far enough away to sound reasonable in his short, business-like cries, not the irritable down-sliding *caw caw*. Blue smells bad. How does she manage it? I hear a mosquito. When do the bats start their night hunting? This time of year, if they wait for dark, it could be nine p.m.

I don't want to think about death.

An airplane headed east, high overhead, sounds almost like part of nature now, but when the Tracker starts up and buzzes away north, it's a noisy pest. Good riddance. Now just some soft *chuck chucks* of a blackbird passing to the south. The osprey arrives in the bay, *yip yip*, still fishing, trying to find food for the family, and the Tracker's wake arrives to caress our shore, playing itself out self-consciously with minor secondary effects. A spider with red and black striped legs drops down her thread outside the screen. A door slams far away.

The clouds have darkened now, no longer a source of light, but the lake and sky are still light, like the white of old enameled china. Every leaf is still, as though everything is waiting. One last boat approaches from the north, entering our channel at the narrows. It's Ervin. His wake reaches the back of the island, but still not a leaf moves. Everything settles back to wait again. Even birds are holding their breaths, but still the evening lives. It should be night but it's not. A bird here or there gets in another word. A boat in Mud Bay can be heard, and then one to the south, but far away. Or is that the first droning of insect sounds? No, the boat sound resolves itself. The Lewises are quiet. No surprises there. A bird in the dark branches above me cheeps every four seconds for a while. The sky is lighter to the north than to the south. A fish, or something, breaks the surface of the lake.

Still the evening hovers. It's now 9:10 and the birds all seem to have one more thing to say. Might as well. And BOOM, the osprey lands hard over toward the now forsaken bass hole, hits and begins to rise, then settles on the water again, then beats its strong wings and rises to the nest. I can't see well enough to know what, if anything, it has caught. Then long silence as day dies.

Now night sounds, a croak, a plop, a fast silent fly-by. Blood thirsty mosquitoes are pressed against the screen. Loons in the channel are beginning their call-of-the-wild yodels now. Exhausted, I fall into bed and sleep like a stone.

22

In the morning, while I'm making coffee, I feel a spasm of need to go to see my mother . . . before realizing my mistake. Sadness grips me now. I've been so very selfish, wanting to hold her dying at bay, to keep it out of my island world. It's not part of the old, cherished story, as though the person who died in Sharbot Lake was entirely different from the mother who shared this cabin with Daddy and me, who would include Hughie for pancakes at breakfast, who loved to fish. Long ago I split my mother in two. My island self still had her childhood mother, the one who haunts my memories of past days here in the cabin. My out-in-the-world self had a different one. I cemented my dad's wife into my rock wall, safe from the wife of a paleoconservative. From an old woman who didn't remember who Phil was—or who I am.

I plug in my laptop and open my journal. As I write now about my mother's death, I feel more guilt than mourning, unless they're the same thing. My deranged thoughts of blocking out the outside world, trying to preserve some kind of island paradise for myself, have been one of my worst self-delusions. That's me. Curled up on my small island, dukes up like the fierce little kingbirds. I've had my defense line drawn, a do-not-disturb sign on the dock, hiding from the self who put her mother out of my Long Island house where I'd intended her to be when I brought her east to be with me until she died. Neither of us could have known that she'd live eleven years, ever more demented. After six years the level of need for care had increased, and it seemed for me a choice between my professional life and my mother, so I gave up my mother. It now seems a heartless thing to have done. This was exactly what had happened to her before, when her parents left her. She'd been told not to cry. Where will I be when I'm helpless and need love more than ever in my life?

I see now that I'm very practiced at grieving for my father, at putting him in first place, at trying to fill his shoes. It's easy to cast a glow upon a deceased parent. He died before the time when parents naturally fade and show themselves to be fallible. My mother stuck around to face my adult judgment, while he was comfortably idolized, sentimentalized, forgiven his sins, even though he had more to be forgiven for. He ran no risk of becoming my ward and being told what to do. "OK, Mommy," my mother would say to me ironically while living under my rule.

No, Dorothea received the gift of long life with its pleasures and rewards, its booby traps and tortures.

* * *

The dogs and I take a morning walk across the farm to Mud Bay, where mica was once mined. The scars in the soil are softened now into the beauty of the forest, marred only by the decaying remains of buildings and rusted equipment. It isn't far across this narrow pass to Mica Point, where they took the mica out to the road and where Ervin now parks his truck.

Returning, I have a good view of my island from the bluff, and as always I feel a surge of love for it, the place where I work harder but am more indulged than anywhere else I go. Through its overhanging foliage I can see sections of the meandering wall I've placed between the lake and the back of the cabin, each rock embraced by me and dedicated to its new role as part of my construction. Humble construction, for sure, but Carl, the fisherman, has chivalrously called my project "The Great Wall of China." Not so chivalrously, he points out that because of my work on the wall for all those years, the most common view he's had of me from the lake was of my butt in the air.

A Section of the Great Wall of China

During lunch on the porch, I remember the hummingbird, but her nest is empty and in disarray. I've missed witnessing new life take flight while my mother's was ending. Suddenly the dirty floor bothers me, and I shoo the dogs out and sweep the cabin. It feels good to be busy. The lake has been sliding over the dam, lowering its level by a foot. It's time to do a little rearranging of nature. I put on a bathing suit, find my work gloves, row to a shoal, and let down the anchor. Gentle waves and sunlight make a perfect rocking day.

I stand in the water beside the boat, pushing it around, looking for good rocks for my wall. Eons ago, retreating glaciers left a variety of broken stones in this area, and I look for hard ones, avoiding sandstone and feldspar, which tend to split under pressure. The only fish I see today are small. They follow me as I sink my arms into the lake, sink them so deep I dip my chin in too, and wrap my fingers around a rock and tug until it gives and I can slide my hands under the slippery under-surface and raise it amidst a cloud of lake dust, tiny particles of leaves and silica floating for a while, reflecting the sun on their slow journey back to the soft sandy lake bottom. Once in a while the minnows swim up and press their little mouths against my leg.

I lift the biggest rocks I can, grinding them against me as I heave them free of the water and up onto the edge of the boat, letting them bump and thump in, just as my dad used to do. Am I still trying to please Daddy? To be like him? Or am I just being myself, the person I've become as a result of being his daughter? My obvious lifelong preference for my father must have hurt my mom. We both loved him, and she loved both of us, but there were times when I forgot to love my mother. I was a *dutiful* daughter.

When the boat has sunk to a few inches from the gunwales, I climb in. As I struggle to row all this weight to the back of the island to unload, I see a bald eagle fly east to west above me like a Homeric omen. Ervin has said that they winter on his farm, eating the leftovers from his slaughtering.

The dogs have been fed and lie beside me as I sit in the rocking chair on the porch. The loons are crossing the channel, calling warbled warnings to their two young ones just like human parents insisting on holding children's hands crossing the road. They stop to feed just off shore in front of the island. These are the loons that the Lewises and I think of as *our* loons because they raise young each year in our bay. They mate for life and live to be twenty-five or thirty years old.

Newly hatched loons, endangered by predators, spend their first few weeks riding on their parents' backs, but these healthy chicks I'm watching this evening are no longer babies. They must be eighteen inches long already. They look like a different species, not black and white but all brown and fluffy, floating feather dusters with heads and necks instead of handles, everything on them brown—beaks, eyes, feathers—unformed as of yet into loons. They float on the surface under the island's overhanging trees while their handsome parents fish the shallow water among a school of minnows. The parents dive and the big ungainly offspring dip their heads under and watch, looking silly and spoiled.

Each parent seems to have a designated chick to attend to, feeding it minnow after minnow, placing them in the young one's bill. The chicks don't swallow the fish right away but drop and play with them in the water, perhaps to position them headfirst. Later I watch with the binoculars as they head back across toward the pass, the chicks diving, but not for long, the parents disappearing under water for longer periods.

When the family stops by Bear Island, a chick cuddles up around one parent, which is grooming and pays no attention, so it swims to the other parent and circles close to its body. Both parents are grooming, so the chick grooms too, lifting its wing and poking its sharp bill among the feathers along its body. Then the second parent rises in the water, beating its wings, and the chick does the same. The parent rises again and practices take-off. Unlike other birds, the bones of the loon are nearly solid, and their strong legs are placed well back on their bodies. This allows them to dive to up to two hundred feet if they need to, but their relatively short wings make it hard to launch into the air. Migration for them is a thousand-mile sprint. It takes this one close to a minute of slapping the water noisily with its wings, then appearing to run on the water, still beating the surface with the tips of its wings, before it can lift itself enough to fly free and circle back, laughing in the air, showing the little loon what loons can do.

Ervin tells me that when the babies can feed themselves, the parents will separate from them for days at a time, then form a flock and fly south ahead of their offspring, leaving them to make the trip alone, apparently never to see them again. Job done.

23

After a late breakfast, I carry a bag of mortar through the bayberry bushes to the worst gap in my wall, pour some of it into the mixing pan, and add lake water. Mixing cement by hand is easier if it's very wet, so some years I've added too much water, and the result is so porous that the wall breaks up when the lake freezes. This time, when I think it's the right consistency, I begin to build. Once started, I enjoy the familiar work. It keeps the dogs interested. They paddle in and out of the lake, surveying as though standing guard. It seems that, because I'm working, even if it's in the same part of the retaining wall all afternoon, they sense it as enterprise.

I choose my rocks carefully to fit as tightly as possible. Once I have a plan, I spread the mixture with my trowel, lower the rock into it, and fill the junctures. If I cemented my childhood mother into these rocks to preserve her, what about me? I've been cementing an important part of myself into it, keeping everything here as it has been all my life, trying to preserve my dad on this island.

While I'm talking to people in New York, even my husband, I feel that I'm alive there as a person who doesn't exist while I'm here. Maybe a Jekyll and Hyde switch where I drop my civilized demeanor for an untamed savagery in the wilderness, where I'm wading through swamps with that knife between my teeth, the image my husband likes to portray when describing me at dinner parties. Here it seems I'm in an X-ray and everything is pared away, leaving just my framework. A strange product of a childhood spent seeing my father kill animals while my mother read me books about a rabbit named Peter, or about Ratty and Mole and a toad who drove a car. Or watching boxing on Friday nights with my dad, followed by Saturday afternoon opera from the Met over the radio with my mother.

I've always been intrigued by Thoreau's admission in *Walden:*

I found myself ranging the woods, like a half-starved hound, with a strange abandonment, seeking some kind of venison which I might devour, and no morsel could have been too savage for me. The wildest scenes had become unaccountably familiar. I found in myself, and still find, an instinct toward a higher, or, as it is named, spiritual life, as do most men, and another toward a primitive rank and savage one, and I reverence them both.

I told my husband that I was happy with myself, and I am, but with all this worry about my admiration for a father who entered the wilderness with a gun, clearly I don't really *know* myself. It used to be important to me to "take after" him. My mother once told me that I walked like him, and when I think of it now, I picture him walking with a joyful swagger. My dad seemed to know who and what he was, take it or leave it. The more he was what he was, good or bad, the more attracted or concerned I was. Until he died, I strove hard to please him and feared his disapproval. How was I different in this from my mother, or Kathrene Pinkerton?

I think about Sylvia Plath's poem "Daddy," a powerful declaration of independence from the idea of a parent lost when she was eight, in which she concludes that she must "kill" Daddy. Far from hating a parent, as she apparently did, I've carried my idea of mine like a chalice, a willing worshipper of what I thought he was, so that I could be daughter to that. One sign of adulthood is the cessation of need for parental support. I lost my father before the turning point, when I still needed him, and I've gone on needing him all my life. Perhaps I've been a child too long, still in the playhouse, clinging to remnants of a security that slipped through my fingers prematurely, returning "home" to Daddy all this time. Maybe I need to "kill" this exclusive veneration of him so I can grow up and acknowledge my debt to my mother.

When I've done enough cementing for one day, I scrape out the last of the mixed cement from the pan, add some water and clean the trowel. As I straighten my tired back and knees, I remember my old father trying to straighten after unloading rocks. He was born 108 years ago.

It occurs to me suddenly that my father went to war in France in 1918, when he was twenty-five years old, and that war might explain his mood swings and the slow burning rages. What had happened twenty-two years before I was born was ancient history to me, and I was never led to be curious about whether my father had seen men or women killed or feared for his own life. On the back dock I sit and think about it.

What we now know as post-traumatic stress disorder, or "shell shock," as it was called in the early twentieth century, could account for much of my dad's behavior, like his trip-wire temper, his occasional withdrawal from us, his use of alcohol to relieve stress. Symptoms of it can recur throughout one's life. His experience during the war was never spoken of in my presence. Aside from that forgotten revolver on the post of his bed, there were no memorabilia lying around the house. That seems to have been a war that combatants didn't want to talk about.

Oh, I remember his singing verses in the bathroom, my mother in the background yelling "Phil!" He'd chuckle, continue shaving, and go on to the next verse. At the time I had no idea what it meant. Just Daddy being funny. I sing the only verse I can remember:

Oh, Mademoiselle from Armentieres,
Parlez-vous?
Oh, Mademoiselle from Armentieres,
Parlez-vous?
She's the hardest working girl in town,
But she makes her living upside down!
Hinky-dinky, parlez-vous?

When I was finally curious enough to ask about his war experience, he was dead. He had talked about the war when my mother would sit up with him after he'd been drinking, but I remember only two things that she imparted to me when I asked. One was that the food the soldiers were given gave him dysentery. He called it "monkey meat." The other was about his pity for a civilian who sold his wedding ring for a loaf of bread. I suspect that my mother was the keeper of much more information.

It could be that, for my dad, my mother and I represented the life he wanted to be able to embrace, but that in some way, at the same time, we were trivial, incapable of consoling him. Maybe, because we would never understand what it was like there in France, instead of healing my dad, the quotidian peace of our lives felt false in the face of the violence he could or should not permit himself to forget. There were times when he seemed to be looking for a fight, setting us up as the enemy, defying us to love him. I've read that survival of war can be simply a continuation of psychic endurance. He must have longed to surrender. Alcohol seemed an inextricable part of the formula for his release.

That didn't make it easy for us. Here in the cabin I have the swimming fins, mask, and snorkel that he bought for me after one of his binges, trying to make it up to me, begging my forgiveness, not for anything specific he'd done to me, but simply for having lost control. I remember him kneeling by the railing upstairs in our house in Kent, apologizing to me, groveling with remorse. He was sorry. Afterward he would try to go on as though it hadn't happened. My mother too would try to get past it, hoping it would all go away, and for long periods, it would. But if you know you may lose control and you know others fear you may, what do you do? Anything to keep control. What you fear most is losing it and being helpless, foolish. You become controlling.

He was never a mean drunk, but there were times when he was not drinking that he seemed to become wound tighter and tighter. His silent treatments were unspoken blows that hurt deeply. We could feel the rage he radiated like heat from a stove. He'd maintain a high degree of cordiality with patients in his office, while we moved around the house as if on broken glass. Something held him back from striking out. I saw him do so only once, two years before he died, when he slapped Dorothea. She just looked him straight in the eye, her eyes tearing up, saying nothing. The look lasted a while. I think they both registered the significance of what had happened, that it wasn't something he'd done before. She never referred to it, nor did I, but after he died, she talked about how poor health in his later years had taken a toll on him, making excuses for him. Both my mother and I were good at remaking the man.

I doubt my mother knew what she was getting into when she married him, but I see now that she handled it very well, listening to him, giving him comfort, not censure for his weakness. As far as I know, she never complained to him about his drinking, probably understanding that he himself wished not to succumb to it and that resistance to it had to come from within him. Far from enabling his addiction, I now believe her love gave him reason not to drink. He depended upon her, and he knew it and told her she'd made his life for him. Her reward for her tolerance came with his positive phases when they'd meet in the hallway and he'd embrace her, pat her on the bottom, and call her "My big sweetheart."

After the death of the strait-laced Puritan she'd married next, she still remembered my dad well enough to tell me that Phil had been the love of her life. What strength it took to practice love. Whether she ever understood the cause of his emotional turmoil or not, she never explained my dad's behavior to me in terms that would imply the post-traumatic stress of combat. If I'm right about it as a cause, it might have contributed to the failure of his first marriage and explain my father's change of purpose in life. According to my mother, while he was in the trenches, another soldier had seizures which increased in frequency, causing him to wish for his chiropractor, who he said could prevent them by adjusting his spine. This seemed to suggest to my father a cathartic new direction, for when he returned to the States, he went to Iowa to study under B. J. Palmer, the son of the founder of chiropractic.

Before he went to war, he'd graduated from the Cleveland School of Art. After the war, he never painted anything again. It's hard for me to remember that he was ever an artist. Soon after he married my mother, she found him feeding all his art work into the furnace. She pleaded with him, in vain, to stop. I have almost no examples of his work, but his sister gave me a chalk drawing of apples from the garden of one of his Irish aunts, done when he was thirteen years old. The aunt had preserved it, hanging in a frame on the wall of her home.

Phil's Apples 1906, age thirteen

24

When my grandparents, Sam and Minnie, retired from their mission, they moved to Kent to be near Dorothea. She seems to have walked a fine line between the views of her dad and those of her husband. I wonder if she'd tried to explain to her distant parents her rushed marriage to a man who held strong beliefs at odds with their life's work, who was divorced and had a teenaged daughter. A man who'd punched his first wife in the face. I have the letters her parents wrote from India at the time. Her mother's letters were full of congratulations and optimism, but Sam's, while loving, were preachy, doing their best to form my parents' views in the ways of the Lord.

Upon meeting Phil, Sam told him that if he ever hit Dorothea, he'd have to answer to him, so he must have gotten wind of the way my father's first marriage ended. Sam was six feet four inches tall, and I can visualize him at that imperious height, trying to intimidate my six-inch shorter but short-fused father. It was much more likely that Phil would punch Sam.

Nevertheless, that summer Dorothea's parents made the trek with them to Bobs Lake, along with her brother Herbert and his wife from Chicago, with their young child. Who thought that up? My father's love for whiskey and his talent for cussing would not have fit in especially well in a Baptist crowd. Perhaps Dorothea hoped the close togetherness would make friends of Phil and her father, but it was not to be. Phil would escape with Hughie, saying they were off hunting woodchucks, which probably meant they had a bottle hidden in a groundhog hole somewhere. He wasn't missed.

Meanwhile, my mother had to sleep and feed seven people in this small, rustic cabin. At the time it had only one bedroom and a day bed in the living room. My parents slept on the floor on the porch. I hope my mother enjoyed her family reunion. At least there were hands to help, something my mother needed because she was pregnant with her first child.

Her parents were there for the botched delivery the following January, 1939, when Dorothea began labor at home in Kent and was taken to a nearby hospital. Because of the mutual bad feelings between the medical profession and chiropractic at that time, Phil had no friends among the medical practitioners in Kent but had arranged with one to deliver the baby. She was allowed to labor for fifty-five hours. As Dorothea weakened, Phil tried to find the doctor but could not, and she labored on . . . and on. When the doctor showed up, he didn't stop it. It wasn't until she said she couldn't go on that the doctor finally took the poor broken baby out by caesarean section. It was a boy that they named Robert Philip. A letter from Minnie to my mother's brother in Chicago describes what happened:

The baby was blue and they put him into an oxygen tent. The next day he was a good color but his head was drawn back. Phil said if the spinal cord showed injury he would die. The next day the baby's back was bowed as well and the following day he died. The doctor had told Dorothea that if he lived he might be a "cripple or an imbecile."

"Then I would rather he died now," she said.

I never saw anything as brave as she is, in all my life. Her calm courage just breaks me all up every time I think of it. Not a tear. We have all tried to be sensible and not rouse her emotions. She always was a little stoic from childhood.

The doctor told her never to try again, as though it was her fault. Minnie and Sam went with my father to the cemetery.

So we took the dear little body in its tiny white casket and put it away under a blanket of pure white snow. It has been the most beautiful winter day that I have ever seen—everything covered with snow which has held all day. It was lovely, a fit emblem of the pure little spirit gone back to its maker. But it was hard to put the little body away in the cold when he was meant for warmth and cuddling. I didn't realize how much he was going to mean to me, say nothing of Dottie and Phil.

I cry when I think about it, but it reminds me of the depth of my mother's strong need and love for me. It's too obvious to say I owe my mother my life, but I was the baby Dorothea felt she was risking her life for. When we both survived *my* delivery, she must have felt as I did when I gave birth to my daughter, the most beautiful thing I'd ever seen. I lived to show Molly the world, to experience it anew through her, to empower her and see her emerge into a life that allowed women a better chance at happiness, and my mother did all that for me.

During the two years that I lived with my mother in Kent after she lost my dad, I believe I was a comfort to her, but it never dawned on me that she might have stoically denied herself strong expressions of grief in order to allow me the freedom to plunge into my college experience. I think now about how she must have felt when I married at nineteen and left her alone while I made a new life. I must have seemed ungrateful, oblivious as I was with regard to the challenges she faced in order to reorder her life.

Every child should be as wanted as I was, yet it's taken me a long time to realize my part of the bargain. If I say, "I'm my father's daughter," it's a curious way of saying more than the obvious. It's a means of exclusion, as though I'm not my mother's daughter. It implies that I have more of my father in me. This way of thinking allowed me to distance myself easily from my mother. It was to forget how she had formed me, devoting herself to my interests, giving me my love of music and books. She taught me to cook, but I have no cherished memories of that, choosing only to remember the one day when my dad advised me to cook bacon slowly.

When he died, I regarded my mother's giving up the island as a sign that she was different from me and from him. The place requires a great deal of work. I thought she was weak, unable to embrace the magnitude of the place, its challenges, its wild beauty. I was too young to see that her unequivocal love for him had required strength. That she'd been my bulwark against his storms, seeing to it that I always knew that I was loved. While he kept us always a bit off balance, I'd depended upon my mother's steadfastness. Actually, I was just following her lead. My love for my father was made possible by her devotion to him.

No one ever thought Dorothea's mother, Minnie, was weak. My grandmother mourned that loss of my mother's first child, which for me begs the question: how did she manage to abandon her own children? Driven by strong Christian faith and a sense of unquestionable purpose, she had courage in facing the hill tribes and tropical diseases of Southern India, not for a winter or a while, but for thirty-four prime years of her life. She followed her husband Sam half-way around the world in order to create a settlement for rehabilitating criminals. I'm in awe of her fortitude. But as I give thought this summer to my mother's life, I've been torn between admiration for Grandma—her courage, her strength, her goodness—and my disbelief that she could have given up her little girl, just seven years old, to be raised by strangers.

Minnie and Sam Bawden

When Sam and Minnie finally left their mission in 1938, the settlement at Kavali had grown into three different towns to manage—Kavali, Bitragunta and Allur—with a combined total of five thousand people. For their work they'd been awarded the Kaiser-i-Hind gold medal by King George V, the highest award that could be awarded to non-British citizens at that time. And yet, while Minnie was running a clinic for strangers on the other side of the globe, her daughter suffered recurring bouts of malaria in the children's home, which the doctors in Granville, Ohio, never having seen such symptoms, could not diagnose. Dorothea's ability to do well in school was affected, and when she failed Latin in her third year of high school, she was finally taken to a diagnostician in Columbus who put her on a regimen of arsenic. Back in Granville she confused the dosage with the frequency and nearly poisoned herself, but finally she had no more fevers . . . and no more excuse for failing Latin.

I have a locket that Minnie wore that opens to two small photos of her children's faces and I imagine her tears. Was this really her choice?

One result of the separation from her parents was that, unlike me, my mother lacked a sense of home to come home to. Everything she ever told me about her life was related offhandedly, but I think my mother must have felt particularly lonely and adrift when thrown out into the world after graduating from Denison University in Granville with a degree in music. She followed a fiancé to Cleveland, only to be jilted. Fortunately, music was a valuable vocation for her all her life. She found jobs teaching music and French until her parents came home on furlough once again. They always enjoyed their reunions, but it meant a painful parting again every seven years.

After Sam and Minnie had sailed for the last time to India, Dorothea met and, within a few months, married Phil. She finally had a home, with a husband and, eventually, a child that she loved. Ours was the home she brought her mother into when Sam died, providing me with a very sweet grandmother. Minnie and Phil had an easy relationship. I surprised myself a few years ago while visiting the Maple Grove cemetery in Granville where Bawdens are buried. When I found the headstone with "Minnie" on it, I was struck by great longing to talk to her.

* * *

In the middle of the night I awake, my hands tingling from my work with the rocks. I change position and lie there sleepless, thinking about my mother and what I did for her and didn't do, tearing myself apart over the awfulness, not so much of her death, but of her life in her last years.

I've never thought about how loss had been such a theme of her life, and not just because of the disappearance of her parents when she was a child. She lost her father, Sam, when he died soon after that summer here on the island. Two years after her mother's death, Dorothea lost Phil. Only two years after that, I left her alone. Within two years of that, she was forced to move when the town of Kent leveraged eminent domain laws to claim her home for a parking lot. She was married in California for only ten years before losing that husband. I hope she felt that she'd come home to me later when I gave her a place in our house, but then I abandoned her once again in the Sharbot Lake Seniors Home. She was always the stoic, never one to beg, making it easy for me to go my own way.

So who am I to judge what my mother chose to do for the rest of her life after losing my father? What makes me think I can judge my grandmother? Like her, *I* abandoned Dorothea. Twice in fact. The first time when I married and moved away just as she'd been widowed, and the second time in the Seniors Home, where she finished her life much as it had begun when she was seven. No, I have no grounds for judging anyone!

In this wash of guilt I realize I'm going to cry. I sit up, turn on the light, reach for the box of tissues, and sob. Blue comes to me, concerned, and I blubber to her about "Grandma" and how I left her here with strangers, helpless and confused. Oh Mother, I'm sorry. Did you know I was sorry I had to disenfranchise you? People said I was the ideal daughter, but you and I know I wasn't. I should have been more patient with you, more of a friend, laughed with you more. Still, I did well for six years until I was desperate and left you here in the Home . . . for five long years. I'm sorry, but I didn't know it would be so *long*. And I'm sorry I didn't explain it to you. I was afraid to tell you that you were never coming home. I hoped your confusion would cover up my terrible betrayal. Instead, it left you more bewildered and rejected.

I'm sorry we had to declare your comfy blue bathrobe too tattered to wear, and that you'd look and look for it, no matter how often I explained why it was gone. You had so few comforts. And the worst injury of all—I separated you from your beloved dear-heart Blue, your friend, your greatest love and solace.

This is why I'm crying tonight, Blue.

**

The shortening summer days are lovely. With the sun nearly touching the western hill, I watch the opposite edge of the world for the annual event when the full moon rises at sunset through the narrow pass directly across the channel. There are whippoor-wills on Timmerman's Island. I can hear them faintly, and a barred owl somewhere on Lewis land monotonously repeating *Who cooks for you? Who cooks for you all?* I keep thinking of things to do in the cabin and come and go. I'm preparing to brush my teeth when I hear two loons yodeling: sounds like *moo—oon*. Something makes me put *loon* and *luna* together and I run out the door. There she is, emerging in the narrow gap between Bear and Mica Islands, a fat and sassy golden globe in a still-blue sky, face features clear, looking warmly across at me. My own Stonehenge. Soon she rises and cools, slimming down.

In her fervent prose Laura Lee Davidson describes it from the height of Mica Island:

. . . I can stand on the very crest of the rock and look eastward to a broad white disk, rising in a sky of tenderest blue, and then westward to the gates of evening, where the sun has sunk behind long golden bars. The heavens are yellow, rose, green and violet, the still water reflects the colors like the inside of a shell, the long lake stretches away, with all its green islands, and I stand in spirit on an exceeding high mountain, seeing the kingdoms of the earth and sky, and the glory of them.

When I've brushed my teeth, I sit looking along a path of silver across the water from my dock to the rock face on Mica Island. The moon is telling me something about the power of reflection. I see now that I had a model of strength for a mother. Strength comes in different forms, and her strength sustained me with a love I didn't fully appreciate. I am so sorry. I was drawn not to her long-term strength of endurance but to the swashbuckling energy posed by the father she'd chosen for me. I will always love him. Because he passed to me his passion for this place, I'm at home in nature, and I realize now that for me nature is religion. I just have to be here to realize it. The moon seems to gather all the elements gradually around me, and, when I'm fully entered into the state of preparedness like a novitiate, she beams this sign for me to know: My mother made me strong. Because of that I'm at home, on an island, on the earth, in the universe.

Later, finding my way to the outhouse without a flashlight, there is no longer a moon path on the dark water but only the clear round reflection, like having two moons to light the night. Split personality that I am, I leave home to come home, two people in parallel existence, rather like the two moons, one reflecting off the lake.

25

The week of Joan's birthday has arrived. On her day off from Sears I pick her up and drive the fifty miles south to Kingston. We laugh at her story about her recent purchase of an answering machine for her telephone. "After it was installed, I woke in the night and sat bolt upright. I could hear a voice in the house. I was so scared my heart started pounding, but after a minute I realized it was my *own* voice. I scared myself!"

We head for the old Prince George Hotel, overlooking the green-water vista of Lake Ontario and Wolfe Island at the mouth of the St. Lawrence, where we can sit out in the breezes from the lake. We finish our lunch with chocolate cake and afterward buy tomatoes, corn, and blueberries at the nearby open-air market. Last before leaving the city, I buy ten bags of Black Earth at Canadian Tire to put inside my wall.

Not far from Joan's house, we stop and pick up my mother's ashes from the funeral home. When I'm alone again, heading back to the lake, I find myself with one of those old hymn tunes worming its way inescapably around in my head: "Come home, come ho-o-ome. Ye who are weary come ho-o-ome." The first thing I want to do is free the ashes from this ugly plastic box. Years ago, in California, she'd wanted to have her ashes scattered over the Pacific Ocean, but I'm taking them home, home to me and to a place where she was happy with Phil. To cradle her in my idea of glory. Forgive me, Mother, for always being in charge.

Behind the cabin, I open the plain blue plastic box and find another box within it, metal, harder to open. Inside it is a plastic bag containing a small amount of grey ash. Dorothea's body, which shrank before my eyes to almost nothing, is now further distilled to this ephemeral token.

Blue comes around the corner of the cabin and, instead of taking the path, steps off to be near me and tramps on the ashes I've just strewn. That's all right; she'll spread them farther as she roams. I like the idea of one's atomic elements spreading everywhere, part of the great cycle. We are, according to Walt Whitman, leaves of grass. We rise and fall to nourish the next crop. "The smallest sprout shows there is really no death . . . And to die is different from what any one supposed, and luckier."

I've always asked that my own ashes be placed on the island behind my retaining wall. Someday my son or daughter will open a small metal box here behind the cabin and wonder at how a body can be reduced to so little. Wonder, indeed, whether these are really *my* remains and not a mixture of ash from the crematory furnace. Intending to scatter them but not wanting to take them in hand, they'll find that most of the ashes fall from the bag in a clump into one place, as though I still single-mindedly show commitment to this place. Later they can tell my grandchildren: "See that Bottle Gentian there? That's where we put Mom."

I rinse the inner box in the lake, then sit on the back dock that Chris and James built. An otter raises her head (I decide to think she's female) out of the lake a few feet from the dock and stares at me. I speak to her: *Hey, who are you?* She continues to look at me curiously, then utters a husky bark. I think we're both saying the same thing. Blue stands to alert and the otter's head disappears. Soon I see her joining some playful companions near the north end of the island.

Now that I'm an orphan, my longing for aloneness seems self-indulgent. I have a family waiting for me. My husband has said he wants to come and spend a few days here and help with the boat and motor when I leave. I'll swim the channel with Blue while he's here to row across with us in case of boat traffic. Someday my grandchildren, Will and Helen, will swim the channel. It's time to look forward, not back.

In the afternoon of my last day alone, I find myself cutting the tips of porcupine quills stuck in the side of a mopey Blue.

We've returned from walking steep rocky wooded slopes on Lewis property above Wilson's Bay. Following one of the well-used paths that Ervin's cows have created in their visits to the water from the hot dry fields above, I worked my way up through the leafy un-dergrowth, carrying a pail with a little water in it. I could hear the dogs nearby crunching leaves underfoot and, like a bird, called to let them know where I was: "I'm going this way." Almost like an answer came a clear piercing *wheeep* from a great crested flycatcher over the hill. It was cool there under the canopy, and it felt good to stretch my legs.

At the top I came to a clearing where Ervin had been cutting firewood. There were no cows in sight. Beyond the stumps in the sunny field I found what I'd been hoping for: a patch of bright gold brown-eyed Susans, their stems long and tough, needing the sharp-bladed penknife I'd brought to cut them.

Already the vicious deer flies had discovered me and were buzzing my head in tight circles. The cows have little defense against them. I believe there must be more mad cows in Canada than there ever were in England, despite that country's struggle with mad cow disease! The dogs stayed near the edge of the woods to try to avoid them. I worked quickly, dropping the cut stems one by one into the water at the bottom of my pail, helicoptering an arm between cuts to keep the flies out of my eyes.

I heard a dog approach, panting, coming right up to me, and there was Blue, trembling, a bunch of porcupine quills in one flank. My reactions came in quick succession: *Oh no!* followed by sympathy for Blue, followed by praise. "Good girl! You weren't hit in the face."

Of course Ring, who accompanied her, had no quills. He sat, panting, aloof, not looking at us as I inspected the damage. My previous dog, an Irish setter named Robin, once took a horrible thicket of quills in her nose, lips, and cheeks, and in those days we didn't know enough to clip the ends off the barbed quills to release the pressure that drives them in. Uncut, they can be fatal if they penetrate soft tissue into the brain. I tried having Ervin hold Robin while I extracted them, and she bit him, so I took her to a vet to have them removed under anesthesia.

Thank goodness Blue had only a few piercing her side. The others came out of her fur in my hand, and I pocketed some as souvenirs, three inches long. When I pulled on the stuck ones, she reached back with concern, so I left them to remove later. Re-crossing the field, I looked to where the dogs had been, and three big porcupines stared back from the branches of a tree. I shook my finger at them, but they were oblivious, as usual.

Poor Blue. Bad things happen, even here in our beloved place. The world's always going to have horrible sticky porcupines, nasty flies, noisy water-skiers, thunder and lightning. We can't defeat them, merely endure, straddle the good and the bad. Judging by what life has up its sleeve, that life that we all value so highly is full of dangers and sorrow and unpredictability and downright horrors as well as pleasures, so we must embrace the whole caboodle, for they contribute to who we are and what we can encompass. Were we promised a rose garden? Yes, we *were*: with thorns, aphids, blackspot, rusts, mildew, necessary pruning . . . and soft splendid blossoms.

* * *

Once cut, the porcupine quills come out easily. The shining daisies fit nicely into an old red and white enameled coffee pot and look at home on the table on the porch. Daisies don't seem to mind being cut. The cabin is clean, everything aired, swept, water brought in, pump going, food provided—I'd like to arrive here with the cabin like this! The roof doesn't leak. I've worked on the rock wall and cut up fallen trees and branches with my chain saw. There have been no visits from raccoons. Thank you, Ring. Next to the landing steps, two magnificent tall swamp milkweeds have exploded in bloom with clusters of bright pink star-shaped flowers.

Good weather for my husband's arrival. He's probably leaving now, grabbing a sandwich to eat in the car, heading for the crowded expressway. He doesn't seem to mind night driving and arriving at the garage in the dark. To him it seems efficient. He'll sleep six hours and awaken here tomorrow, as though he's stolen a day from the travel gods.

I've made a big pot of chili and some cornbread and sit down at the table on the porch to eat. The gulls in the bay have a baby, a puffy brown adolescent as big as his sleek white parents, and they scream at him constantly. The Lewises sit all evening down in Timmerman's Bay and fish in the warm amber light.

It will be dark at 3 a.m. I set my alarm and sleep half dressed, wanting to deny the alarm when it goes off but rising dutifully to put on clothes and turn on my outdoor light. Ring is outside. Blue comes out with me when I go to the outhouse, then obediently goes back to bed when I tell her to. I find my flashlights and an extra life vest. At the last minute I pull an old suede jacket of my dad's off a hanger.

There's only a gentle slap of water against the boats and dock. The motor starts right up and I pull out into the inner channel. Beyond the perimeter of the porch light, the water, sky, and islands are indistinguishable. Where in the morning the sun on the waves makes the channel sparkle, the water is now so black I might be floating on ink. Yet, above me, along the same axis, a band of far distant suns is visible, not *milky* really, but as though the morning's light sparkles have risen high into the sky, a river of stars to cross.

I turn a flashlight on so that I can be seen, but turn it off because all I can see is my own light. And I'm careful not to look directly at the blinding mercury light on Schoolmarm's Point, but I guess the location of the pass relative to it. When I reach the opening, I see Saturn low on the eastern horizon, bright enough to reflect in the water, and head for it through the pass and across the main channel. I guess well in finding Sugar Bush Point too, knowing I'm there when the land blots out the light from the planet.

Rounding the point, I look the length of the bay to see whether there are car lights at the garage. All is dark. I motor well within the bay and anchor, waiting out on the water where mosquitoes are less likely to find me, and watching the tree line for the first sign of bobbing headlights. There's mist lying just above the lake's surface, and I pull the jacket around me to keep out the chill. The boat turns on its anchor and there, higher in the sky than I normally find it at bedtime and bright among the other stars, is Cassiopeia, the Queen, arms extended, ready to receive.

AFTERWORD
2021

Well, that was then, twenty years ago. Not long after I returned to New York and my life of teaching, the world changed. One morning that September, as I was preparing for a class, James called me from his apartment on 11th Street in Manhattan, not far from the World Trade Center. "Mom, turn on the television." Together we watched the second plane fly through the South tower. Then, as Bureau Chief of Gamma, a French photo news agency, he rushed uptown to work. It was three days before he was allowed to return home through a barricade at 14th Street. Homeland Security was founded. The border to Canada was hardened as passports were required for the first time.

For me, however, 2001 was pivotal beyond the 9/11 attack that marks that year as transitional for all of us. That summer, as I'd paddled my canoe around my lovely corner of Bobs Lake, I was the frog in the pot referred to in the movie *An Inconvenient Truth*. The pot was coming to a boil slowly enough that I wasn't yet duly alarmed.

Now I've begun to feel that my little island is less a retreat to solitude and more a part of a dangerously overpopulated and heated-up planet. It has never been more true that "No man is an island," to quote John Donne. Now we have jet skis and 200 horsepower motorboats whizzing around, noisier than I suspect Laura Lee Davidson could have feared they would be. Increasingly, we have drones overhead, with Google Earth spying on every inch of the lake. Occasionally I hear the far-off sound of someone's triggered burglar alarm while trying to hang onto the notion that I'm in the wild. I feel as Annie Dillard did when she said, "In all the history of the world, it has never been so late."

When I was young, it was as though no other world existed

while I was on the lake. Even the long mournful *whooooo whoooo* of
the train, with its distinct rumbling wheel sounds carrying through
the night from Crow Lake two and a half miles away, seemed part
of the wild landscape.

Change is inevitable, of course. Humans have hunted in this
part of Ontario since the end of the last Ice Age, at least 11,000
years ago, according to our local historian, Lloyd Jones. When the
area was first explored by Europeans, there were Iroquois, but
they were run out by Ojibwa who wanted the fur trade with Europeans. The Ojibwa were bought out by the first white settlers who
cut the forests and plowed the land. Then there came the rise of
the middle class and the concomitant rise in consumerism, leisure
time, and technological advance. The descendants of those early
settlers are nearly all gone from the lake now. In recent years there
has been an explosion of demand for home-building property in
pristine areas by affluent Canadians and Americans, resulting in a
steady growth in the number of cottages and homes with water
views around Bobs Lake in areas previously inaccessible by road.

With these changes came an increase in environmental aware-
ness. A lake association, first formed to keep an eye on the viability
of Bobs and Crow Lake for fishing, developed into a watchdog
organization intended to encourage the enforcement of laws to
prevent harmful run-off into the lake, to provide volunteers to
test water quality, to think about safety issues for boating, and,
most importantly, to attempt to stop irresponsible development
around the lake. But support for that group is dwindling.

Bobs Lake is part of a broader lake area that has recently been
named the Frontenac Arch Biosphere Region to encourage sus-
tainable community development and protection of nature for
future generations. In spite of that, the increase in human population inevitably brings adulteration of wildlife habitat and native
plant life, and the changes now are increasingly rapid and destruc-
tive. Almost all people who come here are drawn by the beauty
and the wildness, but the more that come, the less space there is
for the wildlife. Even when we don't mean to intrude upon it, we
just do. The landscaping humans create often replaces native plant

species and conflicts with the needs of wildlife.

Pollution from septic systems, lawn fertilizers, and detergent runoff, together with global warming, create an excess of nutrients, particularly phosphorus and nitrogen, that, in turn, create harmful algae blooms in the lake. We occasionally come across large green clouds of them near the shores. Even when algae blooms are non-toxic, they reduce the oxygen in the water, creating dead zones in the lake. If toxic, they can kill fish and animals and cause illness in humans.

Then there are the invasive species. For years the lake association warned against the advance of zebra mussels brought to the Great Lakes from Russia and spread when boats from those lakes are transferred to smaller inland lakes. I've read that an adult female zebra mussel can produce 30,000 to 40,000 eggs in each reproductive cycle, and over a million each year. They attach themselves to nearly every kind of surface, clogging intake valves, fouling boat hulls and motors, and disrupting the balance of life in the lake. Like all bivalves, these are filter feeders that clarify water, removing contaminants but turning a rich working lake clear. Now they have made it to Bobs Lake. They are very small, but I can see them lining the island's rocks and docks. Their shells are sharp and will cut your feet. As with most invaders, they have no local enemies. There has long been a stable number of fresh-water clams in Bobs Lake. They are not good for eating. At least, not even my dad put them on the table, but they provided a beneficial amount of filtration. Now the tiny zebras will compete for the organisms that these clams need to feed on. In fact, the zebras may starve out most of the life in Bobs Lake before dying off themselves, leaving their sharp little shells behind.

There is also a potential threat of spread from other lakes of round gobies from Eurasia. They feed in complete darkness, giving them an advantage in eating the eggs and young of other fish. They too are prolific breeders. Disease-carrying ticks are doing very well. They crossed the St. Lawrence River on birds. Someone has released crappies into Bobs Lake, a fish good for eating but threatening to the young of other fish, including northern pike and the highly prized walleyes. And human poachers upset the natural cycle. Before bass season begins, I challenge them fishing next to my back dock where there are several bass spawning nests.

"We're not fishing for bass," they say.

"Then why are you casting a few feet from shore where they spawn?"

They refuse to move on.

The irony here is rich. In my family's early days on the lake, we took what we wanted when we wanted it. Thanks in part to my family, I no longer see leopard frogs leaping around on the hill at the Lewises' or hear bullfrogs in Lewis Bay. Now there are rules and understandable reasons for them. We should all know that the Earth's bounty isn't infinitely expendable. I feel each diminution of wildlife deeply. It's as though someone has come and removed my home's furnishings. The warming climate affects wildlife breeding and migration cycles. I believe I see fewer birds, butterflies, and dragonflies than I used to. The little brown bats that used to roost in the boat house and scoop up mosquitos and moths in the evenings are gone. I haven't heard a whippoorwill, woodcock, or bobwhite in years.

Ervin is too old to farm now and is pretty much housebound, with one new knee, one bad one, and pain or numbness from shoulders to fingertips. As I write, the border between the United States and Canada is closed due to the Covid-19 pandemic, so I can't visit with him, but I call him now and then. He observes that summers seem a lot hotter and winter comes later than when he was born, affecting the ice formation and winter fishing. I ask him if he's had a good life, and he says he had the life he wanted.

Ring, one of the great loves of my life, died one spring morning on my island. I'd stopped at Ervin's house in Bolingbroke to get him after his winter outdoors on the chain. He was old and stiff, his white ring of hair matted. Ervin had to lift him into my car. The excitement of being on the island and seeing Blue apparently brought on a heart attack. I couldn't tempt him even with bacon that morning where he'd laid himself out under the trees.

Ervin said, "He died where he wanted to be." Our big Blue died in my arms in New York, deaf and arthritic from her early broken bones.

Joan and I stay in close touch through email. I don't ask her if she's had a good life, but she still hasn't complained. Her mother, Lizzie, died in the Seniors Home a few years after my mother and is buried next to Hughie at Bolingbroke.

I hope to cross the St. Lawrence soon to be with my little island in its poorly state. Trees are becoming endangered there. Many have died due either to above-ground flooding or to invisible undercutting erosion, the water sliding creeping fingers far in under the soil to hollow out support for the roots. Then there are woodpeckers, various blights, gypsy moths, and ice storms to weaken the rest. Someone has sent me a photo of a birch that has fallen, its branches resting on the porch of the cabin. Together, the island and I are growing more and more diminished.

Spring flood

Despite my sadness about all these changes, the sun will still splash the channel with sparkles in the morning and turn the islands green-gold in the evenings. The Milky Way will still stream a highway across the night sky. As I watch for the August moon to rise between the islands, loons will still call to her. I like to think my father would be a conservationist if he were living today. His grandson, James, will be the islander now, with all the energy and passion that inspires.

I've always said that it's my island, but, of course, the truth is that no one can say they own a piece of the wilderness. I haven't owned this island any more than Snake owns it. We are part of the turnover of life on even so small a piece of earth, just part of the epic history of change.

End

Acknowledgments

The Lewises of Bobs Lake, my lifelong friends, have generously shared with me the biographical details of their family. I have sometimes tampered with chronology in this book, which may be noticed by those who are included in my narrative, but everything happened.

Anyone writing about the regional history of Bobs and Crow Lakes in Ontario will be indebted to Lloyd Jones for his book *The Dammed Lakes*, which covers the environmental history of the area. His book has increased my knowledge and expanded my imagination. I also appreciate his encouragement of my own writing project.

Versions of this book have had many readers over the years and I've learned from each one. Thank you to all for honing my sensibilities. I'm particularly grateful to Catherine Wallace, who patiently helped me through the writing of a proposal, to Seth Silverstein for making very old photographs presentable, and to my husband for learning to cook. And many thanks to my editor, Grace Albritton, at Brandylane Publishers for her guidance and expertise.

About the Author

Carolyn McGrath has a degree in classics from the University of Iowa and an M.A. in creative writing from Stony Brook University in N.Y. where she taught for years in the Department of English and directed the Stony Brook $1000 Short Fiction Prize. She now lives in Charlottesville, Virginia, where, before the pandemic, she taught poetry and developmental English and formed a book club in a high security prison for women. In 2020 Canada closed the U.S./Canadian border, causing her to break her record of spending every summer of her life on her island on Bobs Lake.